W9-BJT-105

Sports and All That Jazz

The Percy Hughes Story

Jim Swanson

NODIN PRESS

Copyright 2011 Jim Swanson, All rights reserved. No part of this book may be reproduced in any form whatsoever, by photography or xerography or by any other means, by broadcast or transmission, by translation into any kind of language, nor by recording electronically or otherwise, without permission in writing from the author, except by a reviewer, who may quote brief passages in critical articles or reviews.

Study questions for this book can be found at
www.nodinpress.com/percy-questions

ISBN: 978-1-935666-31-8
Design: John Toren

Library of Congress Cataloging-in-Publication Data

Swanson, Jim, 1938-
Sports and all that jazz : the Percy Hughes story / Jim Swanson.
p. cm.
ISBN 978-1-935666-31-8
1. Hughes, Percy. 2. Jazz musicians--Minnesota--Minneapolis--
Biography. I. Title.
ML419.H84S93 2011
781.65092--dc23
[B]
2011030554

Nodin Press
530 N Third Street
Suite 120
Minneapolis, MN
55401

Sports and All That Jazz

to Percy Hughes, whose music, coaching,
and personal warmth have touched so many

TABLE OF CONTENTS

Foreword by Leigh Kamman   9

  1 Introduction   13

  2 "I Didn't Know About You"   16

  3 The Flame Café   22

  4 Learning to Climb   30

  5 "All Too Soon"   46

  6 "Rocks In My Bed"   50

  7 Where the Home Trees Grow   58

  8 Treed   69

  9 "I'm In Another World"   74

10 "Day Dream"   85

11 Big Band Revival   96

12 Man About Town   101

13 Family: "Love's In My Heart"   103

14 "Pretty and the Wolf"   107

15 Retirement   112

16 Other Trees to Climb   116

17 Broken Branches   121

18 Looking Out Through the Leaves   128

Postscript   139

Foreword

If this book is in your hands now, I urge you to enjoy Jim Swanson's discovery of a friend for life. Swanson came to know Hughes coincidentally, but his fascination grew for this man whose life unfolded within a few miles of his own without his knowledge. Swanson, from a series of interviews, tells of the black music scene that prospered in the Twin Cities after World War II and up to the present day. He describes the struggles of black musicians to break the social barriers that divided the professional music scene and the hatred and fear blacks experienced in the Deep South army camp.

Of special interest is the connection between jazz bands big and small, and how musicians of the Swing era reinvented themselves as dinner-club performers in suburban venues... without losing their "swing."

Alongside Percy's career as a reed man and a much-in-demand bandleader, we also learn of his dedication to a day job delivering mail and his later efforts as an exemplary tennis coach: echoes of Duke Ellington cross-fading with the smack of a tennis racquet against a ball.

Through my many years of experience promoting fine jazz, I regard Hughes as one of the best band leaders and innovators of jazz music in the Twin Cities. And Swanson captures the essence of who he was and continues to be as musician, sportsman, and generous human being.

I invite you to join with Percy Hughes and Jim Swanson in this adventure, share their learning and life experiences, lock in and expand your depth and understanding of the human experience through the years.

Leigh Kamman
The Jazz Image™

Sports and All That Jazz

1

Introduction

On a bright spring morning in 2009, Percy Hughes sat on a kitchen chair, coffee mug in hand, peering across the spacious living area of his ninth floor condo overlooking Woodlake Nature Preserve. The deciduous trees in the neighborhood were still leafless and a soft spring light blanched the white walls of condo. Photos on the wall depicted his early days playing jazz in Twin Cities, his son Percy III and daughter Cheryl, and his wife of thirty-two years, Dolores, known familiarly to all her friends as Dee. A few awards for coaching tennis were scattered here and there.

"Isn't it beautiful here," he mused, giving the remark a lilt that left me wondering whether he meant beautiful "in this condo overlooking the wetland" or beautiful "here on earth."

I sat across from Percy as he peered out from the rim of his mug, a still handsome face under curly black hair, and deep brown eyes. His brown skin was still smooth after eighty-seven years, his mind alert, his soul still alive with music.

As he began to reminisce, Percy's words struck me like pieces of an attractive but challenging puzzle, with earth tones and azure sky intermixed, crystal waters, fishing line, saxophones, clarinets, baseballs, tennis racquets, nightclub gigs, weddings, proms, alumni dances, ballrooms, and love. They leapt across the years, crawled up through albums of photographs, vanished abruptly and then reemerged amid melodies of old standards from the Big Band era. I listened, relying on a tape recorder at first, then discarding it in favor of a notebook into which I was determined to enter the names, places, and events with utter fidelity.

Since that morning I returned to visited with Percy many times, to listen and scribble. Why, you might ask? Because through Percy Hughes I discovered a part of the Twin Cities that seemed to have disappeared behind the locked door of the past. He had the key.

Seventeen years Percy's junior, I came upon the Minneapolis scene after he had already become a legend to aficionados of swing and jazz. Unbeknownst to me, his bands continued to entertain audiences in venues throughout the Twin Cities. Among the younger set his name had faded, along with the great jazz venues such as the Marigold and Prom Ballrooms and the Flame Café where his and other bands had kept the crowds jumping. Yet his story illuminated a great era of jazz in the Twin Cities, and his music exemplified it. It had to be told.

But there is more to Percy's story than that. Some who know little of his career as a legendary jazz musician hold him in the highest regard as an athlete and tennis coach. This second dimension brings added interest and luster to the tale.

It's largely a coincidence that Percy and I became acquainted. When I retired from a career in teaching, I met new people through activities I'd had little time for when fully employed. Like other retirees who play tennis or golf or meet people through biking or bridge clubs, a condo association or

14

through OSHER Learning or extension classes at the university, I became involved in a few new things. My first encounter with Percy Hughes came as a result of my renewed interest in the clarinet. A few weeks after I joined the Normandale Community College Band, I made the acquaintance of a talented reed man a few chairs away from where I sat. It was Percy. As I got to know him, I realized that he represented not only musicianship, but also local history, and character. In short order, I came to believe that an exploration of his life would be eminently worthwhile. I also had an inkling that such an enterprise would help me understand my own life better.

2

"I Didn't Know About You"

In 1956, Percy signed a contract to play regularly at the Point Supper Club in Golden Valley, Minnesota. That same year I graduated from high school in Fairmont, Minnesota, near the Iowa border. During my high school years I developed my musical skills under band director, Dick Scherer. I say "developed" because I was first inspired by my cousin, Denny Scholtes, who was destined to become a fine jazz artist on the sax, clarinet, and flute. By the time I was a sophomore I was first chair clarinetist in the concert band and an alto sax player in the high school swing band. As a junior I was further inspired by Bob Northernscold, a clarinet virtuoso from Mankato who soloed with our high school band during my junior year. I was in awe of his facility and tone. He was the best clarinet player I had ever heard.

At the time I had already developed a love of classical music, pop, swing, and jazz. My LP collection included works of Beethoven, Mozart, Rimsky-Korsakoff, Tchaikowski, Richard Strauss, and other composers that I'd obtained through the Columbia Record Club. I played them again and again on on my Voice of Music HiFi record player. Among my jazz and swing collection were artists Benny Goodman, Artie Shaw, Woody Herman, Billy May, Ray Anthony, Buddy Morrow, the Dorsey Brothers, Les Elgart, and Stan Kenton, to name a few. I had two albums of the Four Freshman, one with Pete Rugalo and five saxes. Sarah Vaughan, Ella Fitzgerald, Louis Armstrong,

Amad Jamal, and Dave Brubeck were also in the mix. During the summer of 1955 I drove with a couple of my friends in our family 1952 power-glide Chevy to the Kato Ballroom in Mankato, Minnesota, to hear the big bands of Billy May, Les Elgart, and Ray Anthony. I loved the syncopated blend of the saxes and the blaring riffs of the trumpets and trombones.

But I had no intention of following my cousin's lead. I had other aspirations that emerged through personal struggles during my college years at St. Olaf. I enjoyed playing in the St. Olaf College band my freshman year, taking lessons from Ruben Haugen, and then switching to the orchestra for the next two years, finally singing in the Viking Chorus my senior year. Still music was to be my avocation not my profession. After four years I emerged with a degree in English education and began my teaching career at Central High School in Albert Lea, Minnesota. My second year in Albert Lea I met Lavonne Johnson who became my wife, and a year later our first daughter, Susan, was born. By this time I was strumming a guitar and singing "The MTA" and "Tijuana Jail." The following summer I sold my clarinet to a budding musician and forgot about that side of my life for forty-four years.

In 1965 my family and I moved to a new house in the

Minneapolis suburb of New Hope, a mile north of where Percy Hughes was playing nightly at The Point Supper Club. In the years that followed we dined with friends there a couple of times. No doubt we danced to his music, though at the time I was oblivious to his world and his history.

In fact, in those days the two Edenic suburbs of New Hope and Golden Valley tended to look askance at the questionable presence of a place that offered black jazz. To many local residents, the place was a nuisance. It needed a watchful eye.

Some residents, of course, were aware of and concerned about racial discrimination. During the late 60's I myself was on the New Hope Human Rights Commission and later the North Suburban Human Relations Council. I was a Northwest Suburbs organizer for the Poor People's March on Washington after the assassination of Martin Luther King, Jr. in 1968. I was even on the Soul Force organized by The Way Youth Center on Plymouth Ave. Still I was a white suburbanite with little peripheral vision. I knew what was going on on the North Side of Minneapolis but not in Golden Valley. To me and most other nearby residents, the Point Supper Club was an invisible oasis of jazz in the middle of a suburban sea. Its audience drew jazz aficionados from all over the Twin Cities, many of them following the tips of radio host Leigh Kamman; Will Jones, "After Last Night" columnist with the *Minneapolis Tribune*; Cedric Adams, the WCCO voice of the Twin Cities and columnist for the same newspaper; and Don Morrison, a reporter and reviewer for the *Minneapolis Star*, who occasionally visited the Point Club to review the cuisine and enjoy the fine music of the Percy Hughes Quartet.

When The Point was gutted by fire in 1973, the *Golden Valley Sun* offered photos of men and women gawking as firemen from the station across the street hosed thousands of gallons of water on the blazing building. The reporter interviewed two bartenders about possible causes of the fire, and a fire department spokesman about the task of firefighting.

No mention was made of The Point's history, its place in the community, the unusual quality of the music it presented, or its likely future. And where was I that day? Probably at home celebrating my thirty-fifth birthday with the family.

All of this is only to say that regardless of my involvement in social justice issues, at the time I, like so many of my fellow citizens, overlooked or misinterpreted what was most important and fateful to others. Times change, sometimes for the better, but things are invariably lost as well. The Big Bands of the thirties and forties carried on with a diminished fan base during the fifties, as bebop captured the imagination of many jazz fans and country music, rock-n-roll, and pop came to dominate the clubs and radio waves. Fine Swing musicians did what they could to continue playing their best music, even if it was widely viewed as mere dinner accompaniment.

The curiosities of youth, training, parents' guidance, teachers' recommendations, personal choice, the path of least resistance, circumstances, coincidences, providence: all of these forces shape the character of an individual. How we become who we are, how our experience forms us, how some parts of us seem to recede and give way to new perspectives and ambitions, how we are sidetracked, momentarily or for years or decades: How are we to know which is the detour and which is the main route? A framework built over years can act as a filter through which our thoughts and perceptions pass, so that we focus on, or overlook, what's immediately in front of us. Experience is like a visual puzzle that teases us into seeing a leafing tree...or two faces looking into each other's eyes.

As we grow older, perhaps we begin to reflect more on how accident and intent have combined to mold our character and shape our lives and interests. One event in my recent past is especially telling. I had wandered down the alley from our house to the annual East Calhoun Community Organization (ECCO) garage sale. There, on a blanket on the lawn, I spotted a vintage clarinet nestled in an open threadbare case. I was drawn to it, and also to another, similar case sitting alongside it. The clarinet was a vintage Paris Selmer with a couple of missing keypads, a Sumner mouthpiece, and a Selmer crystal mouthpiece etched with "Benny Goodman." There were also a couple of ligatures, but no reeds. When I opened the second case I found pads, key oil, cork grease, a small screwdriver, and a couple of scraps of paper: one was a bill from a repair shop in Fargo, North Dakota, dated 1969.

After moments of negotiation, I purchased the two cases for the bargain price of twenty-five dollars and hurried home, strangely eager to glue in a couple of pads, buy some reeds at Music-Go-Around, and give the instrument a toot. It played!— good tone, though it needed some work.

I set the clarinet aside in my study closet, vowing to fix it up and begin practicing soon, but another nine years went by before I took it out again and brought it in to a music shop for an overhaul. Before having the instrument refurbished, I searched on-line for a community band. I considered the Robbinsdale band first, having taught in the district, but the Calhoun Isle Community Band was closer to home, and its website proclaimed the band's two most attractive features: it had been in existence for twenty years, and there was no audition necessary.

So began my musical recovery. Not that I had dismissed music from my life. My appreciation for the classics, good jazz, bluegrass, folk music, and and the fine rock of Simon and Garfunkel, The Beatles, and later Sting, were all part of my eclectic listening. My wife and I enjoyed classical concerts of the Minnesota Orchestra, and I toyed with folk guitar; I was a good listener, an appreciator of artistry, an admirer of the accomplished musicianship to which at one time I had aspired. But I was no longer a musician.

I began practicing from Klosé exercise books and learning some solo pieces I'd kept in a musty box on a basement shelf. My embrasure was flabby, my technique rusty, but like typing or riding a bike, the mind/body connection that had lain dormant for so long returned upon demand.

In talking to a musician friend of mine one afternoon, I heard mention of one Ruben Haugen, a name from my past. During my years at St. Olaf he had given me private lessons. Surprised to discover that he was still teaching, I looked him up and gave him a call. He at least pretended to remember me, "a little short kid" from 1958, and I suspect he really did. For the next year and a half I drove to Burnsville every other month to learn and reminisce. After all these years his teaching was as fresh and meaningful as I had remembered. I began to improve. It seemed as if I was being catapulted back in time to my high school and college years. I was rediscovering my boyhood and resurrecting my musical skills.

During that first year with the Calhoun Isles Community Band, Ralph Koenig, a retired union lawyer who had taken up the clarinet upon retirement, suggested I join the Normandale Community College Band. Soon I sat next to Bob Northernscold, the clarinetist who had inspired me as a youth, four mornings a week. Sitting across from us were sax players Percy Hughes and John Connors.

Octogenarian musicians in the band spoke of Percy in glowing terms, but I had only the vaguest memory of him, or about the Twin Cities jazz scene of that era. As I learned more about Percy, his leadership, his musicianship, and his multifaceted character, I realized I had uncovered a treasure. His own story was extraordinary in itself, and it also revived a part of me that had been lurking in the shadows for decades. Percy Hughes had once been the leader of the most impressive and attended jazz band in the Twin Cities. He was then, and continued to be a gentleman and a man of good will and generosity.

Let me begin with the story of Percy's most glorious era— the years when he was the swing and jazz icon of the Twin Cities.

21

3
The Flame Café

At 9:30 p.m., a young man, recently arrived from Bancroft, Iowa, stepped out of MacPhail School of Music carrying his Selmer alto sax. At the corner of 12th and LaSalle he headed east, turning south again when he reached Nicollet Avenue to continue on his way past the Marigold Ballroom toward the brownstone on Stevens Square where he lived. On that hot July night in 1953, the street outside the Marigold was alive with young white men and women taking a break from dancing; some were smoking and laughing with their women-friends, drinks in hand. Whenever the doors opened to let people in and out, wafts of Big Band music pulsated across the night. Passing cars honked their horns, and someone yelled a greeting to a buddy approaching from across the street.

The young man smiled and kept walking. He was more interested in what lay just three blocks ahead at Nicollet and 16th—the Flame Café, formerly known as the Club Carnival. He had often passed that nightclub before but never entered. Since he was a student, he had no money even for the meager cover charge. Instead, he found his way once again to the open stage door near the back of the building. He stood his sax case on end in the alley and used it as a stool, leaning back against the wall behind him as he listened to the cascading melodies of Percy Hughes and his Orchestra.

His saxophone instructor, Ruben Haugen, had told him that if he wanted to hear what a jazz saxophone should sound

like, he had to listen to Percy at the Flame Café. It took only a single visit to prove the point. He listened with delight to the sax move in and out of the melodies, rising and falling upon the notes as if they were song sparrows alighting and taking flight. He could see the band on stage through the open door, and beyond it the expansive dance floor ringed with tables covered with white cloths. Men and women, elegantly dressed for dinner and dancing, were seated facing the dance floor and the stage. At the Marigold up the street the band was white. Here at the Flame, all but one of the musicians were black. In both places the audience was white.

The youth leaned back against the wall and listened to "Satin Doll" and "Sophisticated Lady." Then Judy Perkins took the stage to sing "It Don't Mean a Thing If It Ain't Got that Swing" and "Poor Butterfly."

At intermission he waited for the musicians to emerge from the club's smoky atmosphere to get a breath or two of fresh air. "I hope you don't mind me listening back here," he asked the piano player Eddie Washington, who was the first to emerge.

"Not at all, not at all," the man relied jovially.

When Percy appeared, the youth complimented him on his sound, stumbling over his words in embarrassment and fully prepared to be dismissed without comment. Instead Percy smiled, shook his hand, and thanked him with a warmth that gave the youth confidence. Then Percy noticed the sax.

"You play?" he asked.

"Yes, I've played some gigs. I'm studying at MacPhail, live close by and often stop by on my way home."

"What's your name?"

"Dennis Scholtes." He reached out his hand to grasp the one extended to him. It was the first time this Iowa boy had ever shaken the hand of a black man and that hand happened to be part of the best saxophone player he had ever heard in person.

"Do you want to come in?" Percy asked, knowing the answer.

"Well, yeh, but I can't afford it."

"Tonight, you're my guest. Come on."

Scholtes sat at the first table among partying couples that Percy has identified as "regulars and great supporters of the band." He listened to the eight-piece group knock out several tunes, including "Don't Get Around Much Any More" and a composition by the band's tenor sax man, Frank Lewis, who also composed and arranged "Knocked Out Blues." Lewis's deft arrangements gave the band the blended sounds of an orchestra twice its size. They sounded like Ellington and Lunceford, but most of all like the Percy Hughes Band. These guys played from paper with dexterity and ease, but each soloist proved capable of re-shaping the tune in his own style. Alongside Percy on alto and Frank Lewis on tenor, were Woodson Bush, a second alto and a master jammer; Dave Goodlow, one of the finest trumpeters around; Harry Anderson, a white guy, on trombone; Bobby Crittenden on drums; Eddie Washington at the keyboard, and Howard Williams on bass.

The group had been formed in 1946 by Irv Williams, but when Irv left for gigs in New York they elected Percy as their leader. Many of the musicians had also played together with the Naval Band at Wold Chamberlain Airport, and had jammed with Percy when he was on furlough from the army. They enjoyed playing together so much that the Twin Cities became their home. When Frank Lewis left the band to go out west, Irv Williams, who had returned from New York in 1952, took his chair on tenor sax for a year and a half, and when drummer Bobby Crittendon became ill, Marv Dahlgren replaced him.

After that glorious night at the Flame Café, Scholtes continued to stop by from time to time, and in years to come he sat in with the Hughes band on special occasions. But for the most part, in that era black venues and white venues remained separate. In fact, the Al Noyes Band performed at the Marigold under the stipulation that it would hire no Negro musicians. Offended as he was, Al Noyes agreed, since the band needed the work.

While discrimination by nightclub and bar managers continued, the musicians themselves were color-blind. Black and white players jammed after hours at black venues like the Clef Club at the corner of Olson Highway and Lyndale Avenue North and also at nearby Howard's Steak House. In fact, when Benny Goodman played at the Prom, he and his bandsmen stopped by Howard's after hours for a little jamming and established a tradition of stop overs for other visiting artists.

Swing and jazz prospered in the Twin Cities during the '50s among young men, many of them just back from the war. They had returned to wives and sweethearts, found good jobs, built small houses in the suburbs like Robbinsdale, Hopkins, Richfield or the more affluent Edina, and started families. But before the family came along, or with the assistance of a baby sitter, these young couples flooded the ballrooms and nightclubs to listen and dance. Their ears had been educated by the big band sounds of Benny Goodman, Tommy and Jimmy Dorsey, and Glenn Miller that they heard on the radio or listened to on long-playing records, and many searched out similar sounds on the home scene. Denny Scholtes was only one of many who soon discovered that at the Flame Café, just down the block from the Marigold, they could hear exciting interpretations of Count Basie, Jimmie Lunceford, and Duke Ellington tunes mixed with the original smooth, tender, energetic arrangements and compositions of Frank Lewis and Percy Hughes, as played by Percy and His Orchestra. And they could also dance there to the best jazz in town.

One couple that frequented The Flame was Ellie Moore and her husband. They loved to spin and jive to the great tunes being performed there, and Ellie, who had established herself in the modeling business, was immediately taken by Percy's suave yet friendly demeanor, his clean-cut look and handsome face. Percy often talked with the guests during intermission, welcoming them, thanking them for coming and taking requests. One night as he passed among the tables, Ellie asked him to sit with them to listen to an offer that might interest him. Curious, Percy took a seat. Ellie introduced herself and then explained that she was interested in using Percy as a model. Young, light-complected black men were in great demand, she explained. With his build and looks, Percy could be on billboards, magazine covers, advertising brochures, and a variety of promos. Percy chuckled at the idea, which had arrived out of the blue, but after a moment's reflection he asked himself: why not? A little extra cash wouldn't hurt and the experience would be worth the effort. And after all, how difficult could it be to sit in front of a camera? So began a modeling career that continued for years.

Alongside its instrumental virtuosity, the Hughes Band offered vocal numbers as well. Dick Mayes added his crooning baritone to several tunes in the band's repertoire, and the beautiful songstress Judy Perkins also captivated the crowd regularly. Having spent two years as lead singer with the International Sweethearts of Rhythm (organized by her sister, Anna Mae Winburn), Judy had come to Minneapolis after World War II just when Percy was beginning to whip his orchestra from the Wold Chamberlain Naval Base bandsmen into shape. It was a perfect fit. Judy's rich, lyrical alto caressed each note with impeccable intonation and timing to produce a sound than many compared to Carmen McRae. Her phrasing added nuance and depth to the already-sophisticated arrangements of Frank Lewis, David Goodlow, and Howard Williams, and when she and Percy teased one another through a melody, they sounded like doves cooing. Together they created a sound that was inviting and distinctly theirs, and it seemed obvious to many in the audience that they would still be harmonizing long after the lights had gone out on the bandstand.

During the band's six years at the Flame Cafe, it had the privilege of backing up artists like Johnny Hodges, lead alto with the Ellington Orchestra; Dizzy Gillespie, widely-recognized as the finest jazz trumpeter of the era; and Charlie Ventura, a fine reed man who had played with Gene Krupa and Charlie Parker. Krupa himself, drummer of Benny Goodman's "Sing, Sing, Sing" fame, also sat in when he was in town. Other notable soloists to perform with Percy's Band included pianist Oscar Peterson, bebop clarinetist Buddy deFranco, trumpeter Clark Terry, and vocalists Sarah Vaughan and Carmen McRae.

When Charlie Ventura sat in, he borrowed Percy's sax and played the most astounding version of "If I Had You," Percy had ever heard. One night Duffy Goodlow, trumpeter with the Hughes band, pulled a fast one on the audience with the help of Dizzie Gillespie. Dizzie was improvising his marvelous bebop behind the screen while Duffy blew his cheeks in a perfect fake. When the number ended and Duffy appeared spent from the effort, Dizzie stepped out and shook his hand. Even then some in the crowd didn't realize what had happened—a tribute to Duffy's artistry.

When the Stan Kenton band was in town, Stan and other members of his band visited the Flame to hear Percy play. At one point an agent for Peggy Lee invited Percy to go on tour with her show, but because the tour took a swing through the South, Percy declined. The hostility he had endured from whites in Louisiana during his army years was something he had no desire to face again.

Percy Hughes Orchestra at the Flame Supper Club. Left to right, Eddie Washington, Dick Mayes, Judy Perkins, Marv Dahlgren, Howard Williams, Percy Hughes, Dave Goodlow, Woodson Bush, Stag Haugesag, Irv Williams.

Most of the young white patrons of the Flame Café were unaware of the fact that the venue they enjoyed visiting five or six nights a week was also the headquarters of one Isadore Blumenfeld, also known as Kid Cann, the head of the local Jewish mafia. Cann had been implicated in the murders of a cab driver, a police officer, and later the journalist Walter Lippmann, who was investigating Cann's underground activities at the time of his death. Cann made certain that the Flame was a respectable front for his operation, and was intolerant of the slightest misdealings at the establishment. Though a man of questionable moral judgment, to say the least, Cann had good taste in music: He was a big fan of Percy Hughes.

One evening during intermission, he motioned to Percy to follow him and his huge body guard, Angus, through the stage door to the back alley. Once they were outside, the dapper gangster turned and thrust a fistful of $100 bills into Percy's hand. "Go ahead, run," he laughed, as Angus slipped his hand inside his suit coat.

Percy took one look at the wad and the disappearing hand, mouth agape, and tossed it back like a live grenade.

"No way. I'm not movin'," he stammered.

Kid Cann doubled over with merriment. Angus withdrew his hand and smiled. Then Kid, or as Percy called him, Fergie, went serious.

"Listen, Percy," he said, "if anyone ever gives you any trouble, you let me know. Listen to me." He wrapped his arm around his shoulder and looked him in the eye. "Don't let anyone cause you grief, you understand?"

Percy nodded. "Thanks," he muttered. "I won't."

"Good, go play us some tunes. Do that Clooney number that Judy sings, that "Tenderly" piece. I like that."

In a few moments Percy introduced, by special request, "Tenderly" with vocalist Judy Perkins to lead off the next set. If a patron had the wits to notice while she sang, he could detect that two or three of the gentlemen moving among the tables were plain clothes officers of the law, looking for any evidence on which to nab the illusive gangster. Percy was grateful for Kid Cann's support, but preferred to remain oblivious of the man's activities. He was a musician, not a "business man." He, like many of the members of the audience, had heard rumors about the man they preferred to ignore. That night, like every other night, Percy drove home in his twelve cylinder, gas guzzling black Lincoln. But it was a night to remember.

The Flame Café years eventually lifted Percy and his band beyond local to national prominence. Throughout the country, jazz critics recognized the Twin Cities as a jazz center because of the outstanding play of the musicians from the Wold Chamberlain Naval Band. Led by Hughes, these musicians became the foundation of good jazz in the Twin Cities for years to come, and inspired young musicians like Dennis Scholtes to learn the art.

4

Learning to Climb

The Early Years

The elm tree on Clinton Avenue South was spreading its branches long before houses began to go up in the neighborhood where Percy Hughes spent his childhood years. Kids came from blocks away just to climb it. From the top you could see the Foshay Tower downtown, more than three miles away. Mickey, the tallest of the neighborhood boys, dared the others (and teased Betty) to scramble up to the tree's first fork—which only he could reach without a boost. With the aid of a single hoist of the climber's foot (often followed by an unceremonious push on the butt) the kids ascended, one after the other, until the tree blossomed with youth. The boys challenged one another to ascend higher, each daring the other onto yet another outstretched limb ten or twenty feet off the ground. The exchanges of bravado were contagious, and none of them would have been able to say later, perhaps, whether they'd been motivated by peer pressure or a personal desire to reach the top. What did any of them need with a higher branch of that elm tree? What was it that compelled them upward to smaller branches, wispier futures, more tenuous hopes?

Percy climbed as high as Mickey, clinging carefully to the topmost branch that swayed above the houses. He had met the challenge, though he remained unconvinced, once he'd reached the top, whether this challenge was really for him. What mattered most was the dare; what mattered was to have something to climb. He was pleased with what he'd done, yet the apex left him empty. Betty smiled at him admiringly from the branch below, which encouraged him but also sent a strange undercurrent of disquiet rippling through him. What a meaningless pursuit this was. How could Betty be impressed by such an inane accomplishment? The exertion of his ascent and the slight vertigo induced by the height sent the adrenaline rushing through him. Where Betty's admiration fit into the emotional ambivalence he was in the grip of he wasn't quite sure.

What he wanted to do more than anything was get down from the tree he'd senselessly conquered and get back out onto the baseball field. He wanted to whip a baseball across the infield to nab a runner at first base who was just an eyelash short of being safe. He swung himself down, arm over leg, sliding along the coarse bark from arched branch to crotch, finally leaping the last eight feet to ground. He raced back into the house through the back door with the other boys and Betty on his tail, but by the time they'd arrived Percy stood in the open doorway with a glum look on his face. "I can't go to the park. I have to practice."

"Aw come on, we need you at third base," someone shouted.

"I'll be there later. Mom says I have to practice. I have a lesson tomorrow with my teacher."

Inside the Hughes home, Percy placed a scratchy 78 rpm recording of Benny Goodman's "One O'clock Jump" on the wind-up Victrola and listened to the watery notes of the clarinet as they trickled into the river of brass. He swayed to the beat, fingering the keys of his instrument as if he were playing the tune himself. And for a moment he was lost in the midst of that magnificent melody, as high and alone as he'd been in the backyard elm, swaying with the wind. He was the music. He was the wind. He was climbing to magical heights.

Suddenly the music stopped. His mother had lifted the arm of the Victrola from the vinyl platter. "I'm listening," she said, with only the slightest touch of irritation.

Percy adjusted the music on the wire metal stand in front of him, adjusted the reed on the mouthpiece of his clarinet, then placed his barely-large-enough fingers painstakingly over the open holes. He sighed in anticipation of the painful reality about to emerge from that metallic instrument. He adjusted his teeth on top of the mouthpiece, cushioned the reed with his lower lip, pulled his lips up tight and blew. The sound poured out as a burp, then a fog, and finally a recognizable G. He closed holes and opened them to "Five foot two, eyes of blue, and oh what those five feet could do." He could hear his mother singing in the kitchen, stopping for each pause, waiting for the next note, but never letting on that the tune wasn't exactly as it was sup-

posed to be. He was fine. Percy was fine. All he needed was practice, practice, practice.

Practice he did, though like so many young musicians, Percy didn't always practice by choice. The clarinet that he had so joyously unwrapped on Christmas Eve five months earlier (it was 1933)

Percy, Sr. and Virginia

had lost its luster. Its holes had become mischievous deterrents to accomplishment, its reed a wooden slab defying vibration. But every day after school, after only a few minutes of shooting baskets, he was required to say goodbye to his friends, go inside, and take up his clarinet. Efforts to beg off, "Aw, Mom, we got a good game going," got him nowhere, and he soon quit fighting it and came to accept practice as a part of his daily routine.

From time to time, when the lessons were dragging, Percy would remember back to his fateful choice on that Christmas Eve. The tree, lit by a myriad of glowing yellow bulbs with tinsel, colored glass balls, and popcorn strings, loomed in the corner of their living room. Under it two packages without name tags, but clearly for Percy and his brother Clayton, lay waiting among other gifts meant for Grandma Little Lu and Grandpa Clarence, Percy Sr. and and Mama Virginia. One of the two was long and narrow, the other was a boxy rectangle. The stench that had accumulated during the day and a half of cooking chitlins had dissipated, and now the aroma of baked ham, collard greens with bacon strips, potatoes, and tender chitlins in onion, garlic, and bell peppers filled the house.

Before dinner everyone gathered around the tree, the adults in chairs, the boys on the floor. Percy, Sr. opened the Bible to Luke 2 and addressed the group. "This is the celebration of our Lord's birth. Let us read the Holy Word." And he began, "In those days there was sent out a decree from Caesar Augustus that all the world should be taxed..."

As his father read the familiar story, Percy stared up at the star aglow on the top of the tree as if he were one of the shepherds—amazed at its appearance, amazed at the story of the babe in the manger who would become the savior of the world. When his father said, "And so it is written," his mother glided to the piano and played one carol after another while the Hughes family sang in harmony—the same carols they would sing the next day during the Christmas morning service at St. Thomas Episcopal church. (Both his parents sang in the choir while the boys invariably sat near the front with Little Lu and Grandpa Clarence.)

The meal followed, ending with Sanka coffee for the adults, Hires root beer for the boys, and apple pie a la mode for dessert. Once the meal had been complete, Percy and Clayton dived toward the Christmas tree, restrained only by their father's voice calling for patience. Hadn't they already been patient beyond tolerance? Still, they waited while the adults opened their presents, no doubt to keep the boys' attention. Percy remembered nothing about those gifts—perhaps jewelry for Mom, a tie for

Dad, perfume for Little Lu, and a hammer for Grandpa, who loved to fix things.

Clayton, being younger than Percy, came next. He chose the boxy rectangle and tore it open. Inside he discovered a brown case with two hinged clasps that he popped loose. Lying on a red velvet bed, a silver cornet gleamed in the Christmas glow.

Percy had waited long enough. He ripped the wrapping paper off his gift like a dog going after a shoe, and opened the case to expose a sparkling silver clarinet.

"Boys, you can decide between yourselves which one you want to play," his father affirmed. "I have made arrangements for you to take lessons from Arthur Lawrence, the best teacher in town."

But fate had been kind, and both boys felt that the instrument they'd chosen blindly was right for them. At the time neither understood what learning an instrument meant in terms of time and effort. Nor had they any idea how much learning to play an instrument would teach them about themselves, about learning itself, about accomplishment, about the joy of music.

That winter Percy's grandfather came to live with them. He was terminally ill, and he died just a week after arriving at the house. To Percy it seemed eerie, peering into the casket at the corpse of a man he'd met for the first time just a few weeks earlier. Inside that casket lay the form, the image of his grandfather, but only that. It was the first time he had been in a funeral home, his first experience with death. Percy was twelve.

As summer rolled around, the basketball hoop on the elm tree in the backyard yielded its magnetism to the large concrete court at Chicago Field. After school Percy and Mickey and Homer Good and Bobby Ingram would race to the park to play Horse or two-on-two, Percy often winning with swish shots from the outside or a dart up the middle for a lay-up. He was good, but smaller than the others. Soon he would discover that his speed and accuracy from the perimeter couldn't

Nicollet Field, where the Minneapolis Millers played.

entirely compensate for his size. By that time he'd developed an entirely new passion: baseball.

Percy had picked up the rudiments of the game playing catch with his dad, but his interest grew stronger when he started playing in the sandlot games at the park. He discovered he could scoop up a grounder and fire it to first base from any spot on the infield with ease. He had a "shotgun for an arm," and could nail a runner even from the third base bag—not many his age could do that! He had found his position.

For Percy and other young baseball players, the minor league Minneapolis Millers offered entertainment and inspiration just a few blocks down the street at Nicollet Field, on Nicollet and Thirty-First Street. He and his buddies shagged balls in the outfield during warm-ups, and during the games they admired the pitching of lefty Jess Petty, the fielding skills of Andy Cohen at second base, and the batting of Ted Williams, Willie Mays, and Joe Hauser, who hit 69 home runs in 1933. (In 1944, when many ballplayers were in the military overseas, Nicollet Field became the home of the Millerettes, a team in the newly-formed All-American Girls Professional Baseball League.

At that time Percy was also in uniform, serving his country.)

In 1933, at the nadir of the Great Depression, few people starved, perhaps, but many knew hunger. Meat, fish, poultry, and many fruits were at a premium—with prices to match. Fresh vegetables abounded in gardens in the summer time, and canned fruits and vegetables stacked the grocer's shelves at low prices. Butter was 28 cents a pound, milk was 10 cents a quart, and a loaf of bread cost a nickel. And Gasoline was 18 cents a gallon. People filled up on bread, milk, and bacon when the pennies were few.

The new President, Franklin D. Roosevelt, had only recently upset Herbert Hoover in a landslide victory, to the consternation of the editors of both the Minneapolis Tribune and Minneapolis Journal. One in four American workers was jobless, and FDR's New Deal had inspired voter with renewed hope for the dismal economy. Only one liberal publication, the *Minneapolis Labor Review*, supported Roosevelt, but its editors focused more on reelecting Floyd B. Olson governor than on the national campaign. It was the time of Campbell's soups, canned spaghetti, Cream of Wheat, and corned beef in a tin. On the radio, people listened to Jack Armstrong, the All American Boy, and Tom Mix sponsored by Ralston. Popular songs of the era included Duke Ellington's "Sophisticated Lady" and Cab Calloway's "Minnie the Moocher."

In the Hughes household music topped all forms of entertainment. Every day the big band recordings of Count Basie, Duke Ellington, Jimmie Lunceford, and Benny Goodman spun on the family Victrola. Before long, Percy, Jr. and Clayton were entertaining guests on their instruments, encouraged by their mother. "Get out your horns, boys. It's time to play," she'd say with a wink and a smile, and her sons would toot out "Poor Butterfly" with Mom at the piano. She loved that song.

Percy, Sr. brought in a good salary as production manager of Speed-O-Lac Company (later Valspar Paint), and as a result, young Percy enjoyed a typical middle-class childhood, complete with bike, baseball glove, tennis racket, basketball, and clarinet, all of which provided opportunities to develop his skills. Yet the Hugheses never forgot their blessings. They attended church and faithfully supported both community and schools. Though the household atmosphere was fun-loving rather than puritanical, both drinking and swearing were strictly forbidden. If a child disobeyed, Mom was known to use a paddle on occasion. Only once did Percy's father take a strap to him. Later in life he couldn't remember what for, but it must have been something terrible.

One day Percy arrived at the Westerling Grocery with a nickel in his hand. When he tried to purchase his favorite candy bar, a Baby Ruth, Mr. Westerling told him that he had orders from Percy's mother not to sell him anything without a note from her. Percy's face paled. He'd been caught. For weeks he'd been extracting a few pennies or a nickel now and again from his mother's purse, which she kept in a bureau drawer. He knew it was the wrong thing to do...but he had to have a candy bar. Clearly his mother had found out. Why hadn't she chastised him? What should he do now? He decided to let the situation ride for a bit. Maybe she'd forget about his transgressions. He certainly knew better than to try the same stunt again—at least not until the coast was clear. So he kept mum. For the next few days the silence was deafening. He thought about confessing, but every time he struggled to work up the nerve, his heart began to pound feverishly and he let it go. Yet his heart also thumped whenever he was in the same room with her, as if it wanted to leap out of his chest and tell her all. Percy was finding out that he was not good at misdeeds. He didn't handle guilt well, either. Aw right, he said to himself, I'll tell her. And he did.

"Mom, I took money from your purse for candy."

"I know," she said. "I was waiting for you to tell me. Thank you. Don't do it anymore."

That was it? No paddle? No paddle. She didn't paddle him. Maybe that's why he remembers that incident more than other, graver offenses for which he felt the sting on his bottom. Anyway, it was over. They both knew it wouldn't happen again.

By such means, Percy and Clayton's parents brought them along, developing a mutuality of respect rather than driving them to "behave" through fear. The boys, in turn, trusted their parents and grandparents to do what was best for them. So when Mom and Dad "made" them practice, it was closer to firm encouragement than demand. Perhaps the demand would have come had they demurred, but they didn't. The same was true of school work and baseball. "Practice, get better, do your homework." Laziness, procrastination, recalcitrance were not acceptable options.

On weekends Percy's parents herded the boys into the family's blue Nash, already packed full of supplies and equipment, and drove out Highways 55 and 25 past Monticello to Fish Lake, where the family owned a cabin they called Bumblebee and a ten-foot aluminum fishing boat. Their father usually spent the weekend doing maintenance work on the property and resting while Percy and Clayton fished. Nothing satisfied them more than sitting in a boat as it rocked gently to the motion of the waves. Sometimes they dropped the anchor, especially in the early spring when the crappies were hitting at a particular spot. More often they drifted, picking up sunnies and bass, at times a northern, on minnows and worms they'd bought at the bait shop in town. Whatever they caught, they had to clean, of course. Percy developed his technique from a neighbor who took a fancy to the boys, and soon he could filet with the experts. Those weekends enchanted the boys, and it may have been while drifting on the water that they sealed their bond as brothers.

Percy attended Warrington Elementary, which stood next door to Bryant Junior High on 38th St. and 4th Ave. in South Minneapolis. He sometimes found himself sitting quietly, almost in a daze, as he scrawled out the letters to sentences about his friend Mickey. "Mickey Good is my best friend," he'd write,

The cabin on Fish Lake.

struggling with the words. He would rest his head on his arm and stare off into space until his eyes rested on the photo of Franklin Delano Roosevelt, the newly elected president, which hung on the wall. But Roosevelt was no help, so his gaze drifted across the room toward the window. That view was obstructed by the curls and soft skin of Betty Marshall, and when he realized what he was looking at, he jerked his eyes back to his paper. He didn't want Betty to think he was staring at her. Besides, he didn't have time for girls, not even Betty Marshall. Once more he drifted. This time to his teacher Mrs. Warden, who was beautiful, so beautiful, he could look at her all day. She and Betty were kindling his life-long interest in beautiful people, though his sensitivity to the beauty that arises from within was only just beginning to develop.

During Percy's years at Bryant Junior High, he played clarinet in the band and took English, math, science, and phy ed courses just like everyone else. After school, during the fall and spring, he hurried over to Chicago Field to shoot baskets, play sandlot baseball, or beat the tennis ball back and forth with Mickey Good on the concrete courts. But his chief love was baseball.

One warm spring day he hung around the field as a team of white players prepared for a game. The shortstop, Billy Wilde, noticed him lolling along the third base line and strolled over to him.

"Hey, kid, you play?" he asked.

"Yeah," Percy affirmed.

"What do you play?"

"Baseball."

"What position?"

"Shortstop. . .or third base."

"Third base? Can you throw the ball?"

"Yeah."

"Let's see." He rifled a shot at Percy to test his reaction. Percy snatched the rising ball and fired it back as hard as he could. Billy Wilde caught it at his navel and chuckled.

"You ain't lyin' kid. What's your name?

"Percy.

"Percy? Where'd you get a name like that?

"From my Pa. He's Percy, Sr. I'm Jr."

"Ok, Jr. Come on, you play third base. Jerry, you take left field."

Jerry was about to protest but thought better of it. He didn't care much since his claim to fame was batting. So Percy found himself playing third base on an integrated team because Billy Wilde didn't care about the color of a good player's skin. Percy never gave it a thought either. Race didn't make a difference in that neighborhood at that time, at least not to the boys. It wasn't until later, when he played on an organized league team, that he realized some were white and others black. The sandlot was integrated. Teams were not.

At the time, 37th Street was the north/south dividing line between white and black neighborhoods in South Minneapolis. The Hughes had lived south of the line, at 3820 5th Avenue

South, for two years when Percy turned 14. He had become a star sandlot infielder.

About that time, Percy, Sr. became the president of the Baker Post Legion Club, and he started a youth baseball team that practiced near the Phyllis Wheatley Center at Sumner Field on the Near North Side. The team consisted of fourteen- to sixteen-year-old "colored" kids. And Percy, Jr. took his third base position on the Baker Post Legion team. Other members of the team included Ward Bell and Billy Marshall, who exchanged fielding and pitching duties; the Breedlove twins, Coselle and Barnell, who covered the outfield and were the team's best hitters; and Ralph Barbie, who squatted behind the plate. The team played against other local legion posts and even won a game once against the Leslie Lawrence St. Paul team.

While the Baker team had some experienced players, many had little skill in stopping a grounder, playing position, or making the appropriate play. Percy wished he could play shortstop or second base, where far more opportunities arose for turning a spectacular double play. More than once he snagged a grounder at third and made the play to second base, only to watch in horror as the second baseman juggled the ball, then threw somewhere in the vicinity of first, but so high that no first baseman under seven feet tall could possibly have reached it. Only once did he field a stinging grounder to third base that resulted in a double play. The second baseman who'd completed the play was more surprised than anyone.

But if Percy caught himself being critical of his teammates, he had only to recall the time when, playing third against the Eau Claire Legion, he lost a high pop fly in the lights and stood chagrined as it dropped, untouched, at his feet as the runner circled behind him and scored.

In spite of losing seasons, Percy and several of his teammates developed into good players. The skills Percy developed would allow him to play in the military Negro League in years to come.

Percy (middle) with two unidentified teammates.

And his time in on the Baker Post Legion team also bore fruit in another way. During one game against St. Paul Lawrence, Percy Sr. invited a neighbor, Albert Allen, to watch his son play at Chicago Field. Allen was considered the finest black tennis player in the Twin Cities at the time, and he'd already noted Percy's athletic skills on the baseball field out of the corner of his eye while batting the tennis ball back and forth on a courts a few yards away. After the game against Lawrence, Allen approached Percy wearing a large smile and said, "I'm going to teach you to play tennis." There didn't seem to be much choice involve—it was a declaration. Allen made the arrangements according to his schedule, and a few days later Percy strolled down to Chicago Field alongside the tennis pro who had insisted on teaching him the finer points of the game.

Allen, a tennis instructor at a local athletic club, started at the beginning, teaching Percy the grip, the forehand and backhand strokes, and the turn of the body as he stepped into the ball. Once Percy had begun to develop a consistent stroke, Allen went on to teach him court positions and the rules of the game. Although he was intrigued, Percy didn't find it easy at first, returning balls hit with a variety of speeds and spins from every angle. His Wilson racquet seemed to have more wood than strings, and it often sent the ball not only over the net, but also over the wire fence beyond the court and down the hill for a block or two.

Though Allen insisted on proper technique, he was also patient and gentle, and Percy came to worship him. He watched his play against other black players, noted his skill at pounding the ball into the back court near the corners, keeping his opponent off balance, often returning to the man's backhand repeatedly until he forced an error and scored a point. But what Percy admired most was how, when Allen's opponent hit a shot shallow, he would drive his return deep and then rush the net, where he would often end the point with a put-away volley or an overhead slam. But Allen kept Percy in the backcourt, perfecting his strokes. Not until he thought Percy was ready did he begin to teach him the art of volleying at the net. Percy learned. Percy learned well. Before long he loved tennis as much as baseball.

He encouraged his friends to play with him and they did. What he enjoyed most, however, was playing against some the stalwart black elders of the game. His first win thrilled him. His second convinced him winning must become a habit. To his chagrin he didn't make the Central High tennis team, but he continued practicing until he could beat such elders as Bill Penn and James Brown—neighbors who were always available for a match.

Percy loved volleying but he hated lobs. Lobs were his nemesis. He rushed the net as often as he could, driving his opponent into the backcourt again and again, only to be undone by a well-placed lob, far too high to reach, that forced him to scramble back to the baseline once again. At 5' 6" he learned that the overhead smash might not be his forte. If his opponent could lob, he stayed back. By the time he was drafted into the Army, Percy could beat all the black players except Albert Allen.

In the midst of the baseball and tennis, Percy made sure he didn't neglect his clarinet. His mother wouldn't have allowed it anyway, and as his skill developed, Percy wouldn't either. He practiced scales and arpeggios from the Klosé series of instructional books and continued lessons with Arthur Lawrence. When summer waned and school started, Percy took his place as first chair clarinetist under band director, Charles Wolford, who was renowned for throwing his baton when he was angry. Percy played his "gray ghost"—the term he used for his metal clarinet—until Chet Groth, a music store owner and friend of the family, gave his father a good deal on an ebonite model. He played that instrument throughout his army days. He learned to read music well and liked it all.

While the entire Hughes family loved jazz, Percy made no attempt at improvisation while in high school. After school and during the summer, he and Clayton played from sheet music in the Phyllis Wheatley Downbeats directed by Jeannette Dorsey—an appropriate name of a jazz leader, although no relation to Tommy and Jimmy. The band performed the music of Ellington, Basie, Miller, and Goodman for community and church events at St. Thomas Episcopal. During this time a legionnaire friend of Percy's father gave him a saxophone in the the key of C, and Margie Pettiford, a saxophone teacher and member of the talented Pettiford family, showed him how to cover the scales on that instrument with considerable grace and ease.

Thus, in his formative years, Percy continued to climb, no longer the branches of a backyard elm tree, but to the heights of his many talents. A black youth that was never mistreated because of his color, Percy developed in the atmosphere of love, guidance, and encouragement provided by his mother, Virginia; his father, Percy, Sr., grandparents Little Lu and Clarence, and mentors such as Arthur Lawrence and Albert Allen. He was the son of a father who had a good job in the middle of the

Depression, of a mother who loved jazz and Christian service, and of a brother with whom he could play duets and chat with across beds before dropping off to sleep at night. Among the many friends with whom he honed his skills and character were Mickey Good, Betty and Billy Marshall, Billy Wilde, the Breedlove twins, Ralph Barbie, Ward Bell, and Clark MacGregor, who would one day become a U.S. congressman.

5

"All Too Soon"

1940-43

When Percy graduated from high school in January of 1940, he joined the crowds of workers searching for jobs and careers in an economy still in the grip of the Great Depression. The ogre of Nazi Germany had raised its ugly head over the continent of Europe, and two years earlier, in the fall of 1938, Hitler had made his first brutal, large-scale assault on the Jews during the savage night of violence known as Krystalnacht. Nazi ambition continued to grow as German troops gobbled up Czechoslovakia, then attacked Poland, inciting France, England, New Zealand, Australia and Canada to declare war on the belligerent power. In 1940 the German army took over Norway and Denmark, Belgium and the Netherlands, while the Soviets, under compact with Germany, occupied Finland and divided up Poland with the Germans. The Nazi army marched on Paris and German U-boats assaulted merchant ships on the Atlantic.

Percy and his friends read about these dire events in the newspapers, but they seemed to be happening on another planet. They viewed the world with a myopic naiveté characteristic of those whose lives are insulated by peace and distance.

Though times were still tough for many in the U. S., the nation's economy had experienced a partial recovery as a result of New Deal initiatives such as the WPA, the Social Security

Act, and the National Labor Relations Act. The average annual income in 1940 was $1,725.00 and a new two-bedroom house cost $3,920. The cost of a new car was $850; a gallon of gas cost 11 cents. Coffee was 85 cents for a two pound bag; eggs, 64 cents per dozen; tomato soup, 23 cents per can. In short, what $100 could buy then would cost $1500 today.

With war on the horizon and work hard to come by, for the young alumni of Central High School the future held a very uncertain promise.

In such an environment, a simple quirk of fate can alter the course of someone's life profoundly. In the summer following graduation, Percy attended an industrial training camp in Shakopee where he learned machine mechanics and multiple drill press operation. One day he severely lacerated his right thumb while operating a machine. The wound healed properly, but the thumb was never quite right, and the accident later had a dramatic impact on Percy's military career.

That fall Percy attended the University of Minnesota, where he majored in "poology" (he says), a reference to the many hours spent at the billiard table rather than studying. He took the required courses, including army ROTC—a discipline that didn't suit him. In spite of his maimed thumb he managed to become an expert marksman.

His other favorite activity was boxing. Billy and Bobby Marshall, black coaches, convinced him to take to the ring where he excelled to the point of reaching the finals in one competition. Later, bigger and better pugilists, more adept at pounding on his skull, convinced Percy to hang up his gloves and stick to pool.

The University didn't hold him long. Because of his drill press training, he got a job with Honeywell making parts for war machines. Percy was one of three black men hired by the company at that time, and he loved both the work and the pay. This might have been his job for years to come if the draft board hadn't interfered.

Percy's life was also moving forward on another front. An attractive young man with olive skin and curly black hair, he had eyes that sparkled like onyx when he smiled. While in high school he'd taken a liking to a pretty young woman, Louise Neal, who lived only three blocks away, but was too shy to initiate a relationship. She took the first step, inviting him to walk with her home, and from that point on their friendship developed naturally. As they matured it grew into attraction: Percy couldn't help but notice Louise's womanly figure. Still, he didn't make advances. She was the guide. She helped him into the excitement of love and passion. For a start, she taught him to dance.

It's easy to imagine Percy and Louise moving to the music of Glenn Miller and Benny Goodman back and forth across the wool carpet in the living room of the Neal home, swaying, swinging, laughing, holding each other with forbidden passion only possible when they were alone together after school. Their love wouldn't be denied, and on a spring Saturday in 1943 at the age of 19 Percy took Louise to be his wife at the home of the minister who lived two doors down the block from the Hughes home. Only close family members witnessed the exchange of vows. The newlyweds took up residence in the Neal home at 3612 4th Avenue South.

The couple had been living together for only a few months when Percy, arriving home from his shift at Honeywell one August afternoon, found a draft notice lying on the living room table. Louise was in the kitchen and didn't hear him come in, but soon discovered him standing with the draft notice in his hand looking off into space.

"Percy," she said. "What are we going to do?"

"What everyone else does, I guess. I go off to war." He said it in a low voice as if he could swallow the truth. "I have to go."

"But I'm pregnant. Doesn't that count for something?"

"No, we're at war. Everybody has to go when called."

Percy thought about his work at Honeywell. He liked it there. He had a good position with possibilities for promotion. The money was good. He could make a good living for his family. He wanted to be at hand when the baby was born, to hold his child in his arms. Maybe he wouldn't come back. Maybe he would never see his child. The Army. Ft. Riley, Kansas. He had never been out of the state. He had never been out of the city except for the family times at the cabin on Fish Lake. He thought of his ROTC training at the University of Minnesota. How annoying it was, how intrusive, how picayune.

Then he thought of his expert marksmanship award. The army could use him. He would serve his country well. For a moment he felt a surge of excitement, a thrill of adventure, as if a door were opening to new possibilities. Something was about to happen in his life for which he hadn't prepared, even though other young men from his graduating class had already been inducted. Now he was one of them and he resolved to make the best of it.

He embraced Louise with strong, confident arms. "It'll be all right," he said.

"When the baby is born you can come and visit. I'll write. I'll call. I'll be okay."

She kissed him and returned to the kitchen.

Percy had two weeks to prepare for the separation. Two weeks to say goodbye. They were poignant, emotional weeks that went by too fast. Suddenly he found himself alone among many heading south in a train from Minneapolis to Ft. Riley, Kansas. He wouldn't see his home again for three years.

6

"Rocks In My Bed"

The War Years

It was hot, and it got hotter as the train whistled its way south past Des Moines toward an enigmatic future. Percy, wearing penny loafers, a yellow short sleeve shirt and khaki trousers, peered through the window at the passing corn fields, and it seemed to him that days were passing by, maybe years, maybe his life. He noticed other young men, equally contemplative, it seemed. Were they, too, thinking about what they were leaving behind? Would they come back to their wives and sweethearts?

Yet Percy also felt a spark of excitement. This unknown future had promise. He would be a good soldier. He would do what was expected of him, no matter the cost. At least he thought so. He imagined himself in the ring sparring with Billy Marshall, a quick jab with the left, another, a block of Billy's right. He felt the adrenaline rush. He danced into position for a right hand smash to his opponent's left cheek. It was a game, a strategy. When it ended, the two men took off their gloves and shook hands. "Nice bout," Billy said. "Thanks. You, too." It was competition. The adrenaline surged not from anger but from the urge to win, to beat the opponent into submission fair and square. But what if his opponent were the enemy? Could he summon the requisite hate to look a man in the eye and beat him to death? Certainly, a long-range shot with his M-1 would be easier, like the exercises in ROTC, with a moving target made of paper and a flag man on the other end waving a direct hit. It wouldn't be like killing another human being. He would shoot at a designated target.

He shook his head to empty his mind of such thoughts. Such imaginings would lead him nowhere. Better to just wait and see. He shifted his thoughts toward music, the Phyllis Wheatley Downbeats, baseball, tennis. No longer "Could he kill a man?" but "Could he play tennis at the camp?"

When the train arrived in Kansas City, a bus was waiting to ferry Percy and several other inductees to the camp. They were mostly black, but a few whites were also in the mix. They chattered greetings, speculated on the accommodations, and engaged in small talk, running on verbal energy that wouldn't burn out until 10 p.m. and lights out.

At Fort Riley, he hardly noticed that the black men lived in a six-man hut overlooking the long, white barracks where the white draftees enjoyed the luxury of toilets and showers. There was no integration here. "Separate but equal" was still the rule of the day, and the "equal" part was definitely a misnomer, but it didn't seem to matter to Percy. He would be staying here only as long as it took for his classification.

To his amazement, his superiors judged him unsuitable for military action because of his maimed right thumb. Equally surprising, they were less interested in his expert marksmanship than in the fact that he had studied typing in junior high. Due to this fortuitous fact, Percy was assigned as Company Clerk. The title sounded impressive, and the position came with privileges unavailable to most young soldiers.

Soon the army transferred him to Fort Leavenworth. Again, blacks and whites lived in separate quarters, the blacks, servants to the whites. They made their beds, did their laundry, and cleaned their barracks. Percy, however, typed letters and documents for white officers and for white students at the officers' training school.

Three separate facilities: the Negro quarters, the white barracks for the officers' training school, and the federal prison, spread across the flat Kansas terrain. Convicts and black soldiers exercised at different times on a large athletic field. Percy played baseball for the Negro army team that often competed against the prison team. To his delight, he also cooked up a series of preseason exhibition games with the Kansas City Monarchs, a team in the Negro League. The Monarchs were good. Two men on their roster—Satchel Paige and Jackie Robinson—would later became known in every household in America.

Percy was a talented ballplayer himself, and the Monarchs' stellar play inspired him to take the game more seriously. But his love of music was given an even greater impetus by the arrival of a few black draftees to play in the Negro Ground Force Army Band. These young men had already become prominent figures in the world of Swing. Among them were saxophonist Russell Procope, who played with Duke Ellington; guitarist Irwin Ashby from the Nat King Cole band; clarinetist Chauncey Haughton, who had worked with both Ellington and Count Basie. Soon Percy found himself playing clarinet and saxophone alongside these musicians, performing for field day and officers club events. They cut loose on fast Swing and blues numbers like "How High the Moon," "Perdido," "C-jam Blues," and "Sweet Georgia Brown." After hours the guys often got together, white and black musicians from segregated bands, and "jammed." Among musicians, music counted more than race. The white players eagerly picked up the tunes and techniques improvised by the black players and Percy learned from both.

Because of his position as company clerk, Percy had the privilege of using a jeep for transportation and the responsibility for typing evening and weekend passes. He could always write passes for himself but found that no one censured him for handing out a few to his friends and fellow musicians. On

The 32nd Infantry Army Band

a Saturday night they'd roar into 18th and Vine in Kansas City to listen to the jazz groups that had arrived from New Orleans. Kansas City jazz had developed a style of its own, too, and nowhere outside of New York Harlem and Chicago was the jazz scene more prominent. Here a young musician, Jay McShann, had started a band in the late thirties that nurtured a blossoming Charlie Parker. Parker went on to make a name for himself in New York, but he returned to Kansas City for a few gigs in 1943, and Percy and friends were there to hear him play. With such inspiration and the tunes of Ellington and Basie as his instruction, Percy practiced whenever he could. Though still a novice in many ways, he got the opportunity to jam with McShann, and his confidence got a boost when McShann said to him, "You're going to be all right." Those words of encouragement drove him to keep practicing, just as his mother's urging had years earlier.

Years later, when the baseball league offered him an opportunity to play professionally for the Kansas City Monarchs, he had to decide between sport and music. He chose music.

During his time at Forts Riley and Leavenworth, Percy didn't pay much attention to the disparity in white and black living conditions or the "separate but equal" misnomer. There seemed to be no hostility among the soldiers, certainly not among the white and black musicians, who managed to get together after hours to play some tunes. The segregated world seemed benign to him. Could it be that he was convinced of the order of things? That Afro-Americans were relegated to inferior roles by design? That it was natural to be with your own kind? Didn't he notice the difference in privilege, opportunity, and position?

Such issues became more glaring when Percy and the Army Ground Force Band were transferred in the summer of 1944 to hot, humid, mosquito-infested Camp Livingston, Louisiana. An incident two years earlier had been widely reported, though there were several versions of the event in circulation. By one account, a black soldier walking on Lee Street in Alexandria, a neighboring town, refused to step into the gutter as he met a white man. A white MP, seeing this as insubordination, beat the black soldier with his night stick nearly to death. Black soldiers in town for a weekend pass retaliated. White MPs swooped in like hawks, shooting into the the crowd of Negroes, scattering them and leaving six dead.

Another account had it that the incident started in the bars crowded with belligerent, drunken sailors, white and black; the brawl took on a life of its own that that had to be squelched by the military. Whether townspeople were involved was never firmly established. In any case, a fog of prejudice pervaded the city, and the misty bar and night club scene on Lee Street, where on weekends blacks and whites drank and caroused together, was an invitation to confrontation.

In Louisiana black people had "to know their place" or they could expect serious trouble. Black soldiers, no matter what their rank, had to take to the street when meeting any white person; they had to ride in the back of the bus, drink from the "colored" fountains, and use the "colored" public rest rooms. They were restricted from many public restaurants and bars. At the camp, rumors circulated about the "hanging tree" where blacks had been lynched for disobedience or for devil worship. White officers meted out punishment "just like a lynch mob with a Neggro (sic) to hang." Some rumored that underground tunnels provided a network for secret activities that no one dared to discuss.

Percy heard about the riot shortly after arriving at Camp Livingston, but he had not personally experienced such prejudicial hatred until one evening when he and two companions were walking down Lee Street themselves. Suddenly a sedan sped by from which white men showered the street with bullets. Luckily they missed their mark as black people scurried for shelter.

That was the first time Percy felt it dangerous to be a black man. Fear welled up in him. Anger. What could he do? It had nothing to do with his behavior. These whites hated him for his color. The anger turned to rage, festered inside him like boiling lava. He hated the feeling. He hated those white men. He hated himself for feeling such hatred. It wasn't Christian. That feeling went against everything he had been taught. Now all he could think about was escaping from this horrible place, this town, this camp, this mosquito- and snake-infested swamp of prejudice and discrimination. But he couldn't—not until he was discharged. In the meantime, he would stay in camp. No more weekend passes into town. Instead he patronized the PX for his needs. He felt cowardly, fearful. He had trouble distinguishing between rumor and fact. One day on bivouac he watched while a young Negro soldier, bitten by a water moccasin, lay without medical treatment a short distance from camp. He could hear the moans as the man's life slipped away. This never would have happened to a white soldier. Percy was living daily in a dark night.

But rays of sunlight occasionally burst through, especially when he was playing music with the friends who had arrived with him from Ft. Leavenworth. They played for officers' events and parades, though whites and blacks held no jam sessions after hours. The white musicians here were not about to cross racial lines to play music. They stayed with their own band, their own kind. For Percy it was music that kept the dark feelings at bay. Music helped him survive.

Another ray of sunlight arrived when his wife, Louise, visited him for the first time, accompanied by his six-month-old son, Percy III. When he laid eyes on little Perc and his wife for the first time in a year, joy returned to him. Their brief presence healed him like music. For one week, he spent every moment he could with them, though he feared for their safety when they were apart. They stayed together that week in a company facility that accommodated such visitations, then sadly said their goodbyes. From then on the image of little Perc smiled him to sleep at night.

Percy and Clayton during the war years.

A few months later Percy was transferred to Fort Huachuca, near Sierra Vista, Arizona, where he continued to serve as company clerk with a jeep at his disposal. Once more he played sax and clarinet with his Army Ground Force Band buddies. But the living conditions there were better than before. The officers for whom he typed memos and orders were civil, decent men, who allowed him to forget the abuses he experienced in Louisiana. By now Percy was an accomplished musician, improvising with the best of them. On weekend passes, he and his friends would occasionally skirt south of the border to the exotic towns of Naco and Agua Prieta, Mexico, which offered entertainment and shopping. Agua Prieta had only recently emerged from the Sonoran desert, blossoming into a thriving tourist destination for American visitors. New bars, shops, and markets catered to adventurous soldiers who arrived every weekend looking for a good time, with their pay checks burning holes in their pockets. What a contrast to Alexandria!

For Percy, Fort Huachuca salved his wounds and helped him to look back fondly on his years in the army. After a year there, he was transferred to Camp McCoy, Wisconsin, where on Feb. 2, 1946, he was discharged, a noted marksman, from the 204th Army Ground Force Division, rank Tech 5th Grade. He had entered the army with little idea of what he would become, with little awareness of the ugliness of prejudice. He left it a musician who knew of those who hated him for his color and of those for whom color made no difference.

7

Where the Home Trees Grow

Domestic Life and Music

When Percy was discharged from Camp McCoy, he returned to his wife, Louise, and three-year-old Percy III. At first the Hughes family made do in the upper duplex of the Neal house at 3615 4th Avenue South, but soon after Percy arrived back home Louise's mother Carrie Neal purchased a new duplex a few blocks way at 3948 5th Avenue South, and Percy, Louise, and Percy III moved into the upper unit. During this period Percy assisted his mother-in-law, whom he adored, with the Neal Funeral Home business. During Percy's time in uniform Squire Neal, Carrie's husband, had operated the funeral home in St. Paul, while she managed the one at Washington and Cedar in Minneapolis. After the Neals divorced, Carrie continued to run the Minneapolis site at 2435 4th Avenue South with Percy's assistance. Within a year Percy obtained his license as a funeral director from the University of Minnesota and began to supervise the business, allowing Mrs. Neal to reduce her work load.

Percy's license qualified him to assist with embalming but not to perform that part of the operation on his own. He soon discovered that he had a knack for applying the cosmetics, and with his personal touch the deceased looked their best. Percy felt deep empathy for the bereaved and was soon adept at comforting those in sorrow.

On one occasion, Percy prepared a young man in his 40s who had died of multiple injuries in a automobile accident. To repair the deep wounds to the face and head required all of his skill and care, but he wanted the young widow to view her husband just as she remembered him. She approached, saw her husband lying utterly lifelike in the casket, and swooned into Percy's arms.

The emotional trauma of witnessing so much suffering took its toll, however, and it was compounded by the fact that many of his black brothers and sisters didn't have the money to afford a proper funeral for their loved ones. Percy did what he could to help, but his means were limited. Eventually these burdens became too heavy to bear, and feeling he could never do enough for his clients, Percy resigned in 1951, leaving his mother-in-law to run the business on her own.

During the war years women had found a place in the work force and black men served overseas in the military. After the war, many were less than eager to return to their previous position as second class citizens. They lent their support to young leaders like Hubert H. Humphrey, who defeated incumbent Marvin Kline to become mayor of Minneapolis in 1946. Aided more by his eloquent voice than his authority as mayor, Humphrey did much to improve race relations and economic conditions for Afro-Americans in Minnesota. For example, he joined with the Urban League, the Jewish Community Relations Council, and other civil rights advocates to establish a Council of Human Relations that challenged the Housing Authority, restauranteurs, night club, and hotel managers to treat people of all races and religions equally.

During Percy's years at the funeral home Louise worked for a local black newspaper, *The Spokesman*, which supported Humphrey in his mayoral run and his later civil rights initiatives. Humphrey's untiring campaign for economic justice and fairness also drew the support of many blacks, Jews, and local religious leaders such as Rev. Rueben Youngdahl of Mt. Olivet Lutheran Church, whose brother Luther was elected governor the following year.

During his last days at the Neal Funeral Home, Percy learned of an opening at the U. S. Postal Service from a trumpeter friend of his, Jackie Coan, whose father was Postmaster of the local branch. He accepted the job as a substitute mail carrier and before long was given a full-time route covering the territory in South Minneapolis between 39th and 43rd streets, and Lyndale and Dupont avenues. (Minneapolis Laker basketball great Vern Mickelson was among the residents to whom he delivered mail daily.) Percy loved the work, except for the neighborhood dogs, which seemed to have an inborn antipathy for uniforms. He enjoyed the casual conversations with residents, and over the years he developed more than a few lasting friendships.

While his day job provided him with adventure, friendships, and personal growth, after hours he lived for his music. Within weeks of returning from the service, Percy had rejoined his old friends from the old Wold Chamberlain Naval Base and begun to search out venues for their music. Two of the more prestigious venues, the Prom and the Marigold ballrooms, were definitely out: they didn't allow black musicians to perform on their stages.

At the time Irv Williams was the ad hoc leader of the group. He had arrived in Minneapolis on a warm August evening in 1942, suitcase in hand. It was a Friday, and he was eager to take up his assignment as a sailor at Wold Chamberlain Naval Base in St. Paul the following Monday. He strolled into the Nicollet Hotel, across the street from the Great Northern Terminal, to get a room, only to be told that the hotel was full. He tried another hotel a little further down Hennepin Avenue with the same result. He was waiting for the traffic light to turn on Seventh and Hennepin when a passing black man queried, "Are you looking for a room?"

"Yes, sir, I am," Irv replied.

"Well, you ain't gonna find a hotel in town that'll put up a Neee-groo," the stranger said, pronouncing the word to underscore its more derogatory connotations. "If you want a place, go to LaSalle and Ninth, just two blocks down and one to the left. That's the YMCA. They'll take ya in."

Irv took the man's advice, found the accommodations suitable and the management respectful, and was soon out on the street again, attempting to locate a local jazz joint. His first few inquiries met with blank stares, but eventually someone directed him to the North Side where, he was told, black and white musicians jammed at Harold's Steak House and the Blue Note. He took a taxi in that direction and spotted the Elm Rest Club at Lyndale and Sixth. He'd hit the jackpot. Inside, bassist Oscar Pettiford was improvising with a group of guys. Irv just listened as Oscar and his friends improvised into the wee hours of the morning.

When the club finally closed for the night and Irv inquired about transportation back to the Y, Oscar offered him a ride. On that ride a friendship developed, and with it an opportunity to jam with Oscar, Frank Hines, and Walter Lear the next night. Oscar, he soon learned, was from a talented family whose father had become the mainstay at El Patio and the Cotton Club. Oscar's sister Margaret had taught Percy jazz sax in his early years at Phyllis Wheatley House. Oscar later went on to make a name for himself with the Woody Herman band. But at the time, all that mattered to Irv was that he'd found a group of very talented local musicians to jam with when he got leave from the naval base.

By the time Percy arrived home from Camp McCoy in 1946, Irv had become a mainstay of the local jazz scene in Minneapolis, and was considered the unofficial leader of the Navy band. But just before Percy arrived, Irv left to play with Billy Eckstine in New York. One evening when the Navy band was playing at the Elk's Rest Club, the members asked Percy to step outside for a few moments. They wanted to discuss something. Percy had no idea what was going on until the guys called him back in and told him they'd chosen him as their new band leader. From that night on, it was Percy Hughes and His Orchestra, and under that moniker the band would become the most famous and most admired in the Twin Cities.

The originals from that ex-Navy group were Dave (Duffy) Goodlow on trumpet, Pete Wilson on trombone, Woodson Bush on alto, Howard Williams on bass, and Eddie Washington on piano. When Irv returned to the Twin Cities in 1952, he put together a new quartet of his own and played gigs all over town. He played with Percy's band at the Flame in '53 and '54, then went back to fronting his own quartet.

After auditioning for black club owner Dick Mann, the new band, Percy Hughes and His Orchestra, performed nightly at the Treasure Inn, located at the intersection of Rice Street and Wheelock Parkway in St. Paul. There his band's reputation surged among young blacks. As the word spread to white

The Treasure Island band. From left, Bobby Mendenhall (trombone) ,Percy, Dave Goodlow (trumpet), Bobby Crittlenden (drums), Woodspon Bush (alto), Howard Williams (bass), Frank Lewis (tenor) Eddie Washington (piano), Judy Perkins.

college students in the area, the place jumped even more. Percy commented, "It was a place where whites and blacks played together in brotherly love."

Still, people continued to stereotype ethnic groups based on the unseemly antics of a few, and many whites viewed black musicians as rowdy, likely to cause trouble and end up on the wrong side of the law. But for those who could see through such crude stereotypes, the Percy Hughes band offered the refined magic of jazz.

Whites would have been much slower in discovering Percy, however, if it hadn't been for the efforts of Leigh Kamman of WLOL, who promoted him and other jazz artists on his afternoon show "Swing Club." During an outdoor concert at Coffman Memorial at the University of Minnesota in the summer session in 1946, Percy played with his ex-Navy band members while Leigh Kamman listened. After the concert Percy and bandmen met Leigh and expressed their gratitude for his promotions. Subsequently, Leigh sponsored the group at the Calhoun Beach Hotel and the Radisson in downtown Minneapolis and promoted them on the "We Call It Jazz Show." Kammen recognized that the group's musical style was special. It was also through his continued support that Treasure Inn became a hangout for white college kids from the University of Minnesota, Hamline, Macalaster, St. Thomas and Augsburg. So many flocked to the Inn, in fact, that the floor of this house-turned -nightclub had to be shored up to keep it from collapsing.

Percy said during one of our interviews, "It was Leigh Kamman that created the Percy Hughes Band." Though Leigh never took up an instrument himself, he became fascinated with jazz at the age of twelve. His family was vacationing at the Lake Minnewaska Silver Beach Resort near Glenwood, and he heard a 78-rpm recording of "Stormy Weather" sung by Ivy Anderson with the Duke Ellington band and Andy Kirk and his Clouds of Joy Band. That was 1935.

Leigh Kamman (center) next to Judy Perkins with Percy in the background.

Kammen's enthusiasm for the form eventually led to the "We Call It Jazz" radio program, which was on the air between 1946 and 1950. The live show ran on Sunday evenings at 9 p.m. at a variety of locations, including The Calhoun Beach Club, the Radisson, and Treasure Inn. Several bands and combos performed during the evening, and the Percy Hughes band was often one of them.

At a Treasure Inn concert on April 4, 1948, the first half of the program featured "Percy Hughes and His Orchestra with Judy Perkins" and the second "The Percy Hughes Orchestra featuring Johnny Bothwell." At the time, Bothwell was considered the best white sax player in the business—a white Johnny Hodges. While many bar and ballroom managers refused to hire Percy's group, Leigh Kamman's promotion swelled attendance for the performances he did land and brought him jobs on college campuses. Of Leigh, Percy says, "His instrument is his microphone...There's only one voice like it in this world."

When not delivering mail or performing into the wee hours, Percy also found the time to attend the Minneapolis School of Music on the GI Bill and take voice lessons at MacPhail. Unfortunately, his Treasure Inn gig came to abrupt end after two and half solid years. One night while the Hughes band was in the middle of a set, a loud argument erupted near the back of the room and a shot rang out, then another. Percy ducked behind his music stand, as if the flimsy prop could save him. When the smoke cleared, Percy's good friend Felix Clardy lay dying in a pool of blood with gunshots to the chest. It was a traumatic moment for Percy. "What for?" he muttered in disbelief. Shortly thereafter the Inn was forced to close, its reputation irreversibly damaged.

Such isolated events could have a profound effect on a black musician's career, because there were so few venues open to him in the first place, as Nell Dodson Russell made clear in her column "The Way I See It." Percy considered himself lucky

The orchestra at Snyder's Restaurant

to find steady work at Snyders' Restaurant downtown on Sixth Street across from Juster Brothers' Men's Clothing. It was well known that the first floor of the club was used for dining and music, while the second floor offered ping pong, pool...and illegal professional gambling. Percy welcomed the opportunity to play regularly in front of an appreciative audience. What took place in backrooms above his head was out of his control.

In the summer of those same years, 1948 and 49, Percy and his band found work at Bar Harbor on Gull Lake north of Brainard, an entertainment (and gambling) hotspot at the time, and a popular woodland night club with live music even today.

By the early 1950s, with the help of Leigh Kamman's promotions, Percy Hughes and His Orchestra had become the most popular local night club band in the Twin Cities, and the Flame Café the most highly rated jazz venue. The dance era was still in full swing and the Twin Cities, along with Chicago and Kansas City, was a hub of jazz, swing, and ballroom dancing activity. Percy Hughes was at the center of it all: it was his golden era. As early as 1947 he began playing at private parties such as the ball at the Nicollet Hotel in 1947 for the Minneapolis Mayor Hubert Humphrey and a house party at the home of Judge Miles Lord.

Percy with Hubert H. Humphrey (left) and Justice Miles Lord.

To sustain this level of appeal, Percy rehearsed his band diligently, working up the arrangements of Twin Cities musicians Frank Lewis, Duffy Goodlow, and Howard Williams until the band had put its distinctive stamp on them. Aficionados could easily identify the "sound" of the Percy Hughes Orchestra. That's what they came to hear. But it wasn't easy, alongside a day job and family responsibilities, to keep a band in top form and performing regularly in the evenings. Not to mention the demands of being the band's soloing clarinetist, alto, tenor, and bari sax man as well.

Louise attended Percy's gigs from time to time while her mother took care of Percy III and their infant daughter, Cheryl, who arrived on December 13, 1949; but Percy was burning the candle at both ends, and Louise found it increasingly difficult to cope with the chaos and loneliness. She needed more. She needed a husband.

Percy made an effort to be a family man, heading home after his gigs rather than jamming at other clubs as some of his band members did. Still, the young lovers felt their lives growing apart. Often Percy came home to a wife who turned away from him when he lay down beside her. Loneliness lived with them both like an unwelcome, distant relative. They disagreed about family time, responsibilities and personal needs.

Cheryl remembers driving with her mother to The Flame Café to drop off her father for the evening gigs. She also remembers participating in style shows as a child. Her mother taught her how to walk and twirl at the appropriate time while she looked on proudly. Percy would sing a note when his daughter appeared on stage to indicate, "That's my daughter."

The band would sometimes practice at the Neal home at 39th and 5th where the Hughes lived upstairs. Cheryl recalls that the family dog, Ditto, loved to add to the music in a high-pitched howl, to everyone's joy and consternation. When preparing for rehearsal, Percy often sat at the kitchen table with stick pen and ink well making notes for the players on the score. Much to her father's chagrin, Cheryl, always willing to help, would add her own scribbles to the charts. They may have been charming, but few of them added much to the band's styling of a piece.

Alongside such pleasant memories, Cheryl also remembers family arguments so heated she was forced to plug her ears. They were usually about her dad not being at home and her mother not having a life. Perhaps her parents married too young. They'd grown up together and fell into marriage as easily as jumping into a swimming pool. They knew each other too well—but perhaps not well at all. It had never occurred to them that their lifestyles might become incompatible. Her mother cried often, and during these stressful times Cheryl felt more secure sleeping with Grandmother Neal in her bed.

When Louise met a mortician who had worked with the Neals, her life made a final turn away from Percy. By this time Percy, too, had developed another interest: Judy Perkins, the singer in his band. When Judy joined the band she had a boyfriend, but as melodies and counterpoint evolved into something more than musical conversation between the two of them, Percy began to command the greater part of her affection. His saxophone responded to every note she sang, and she sang every song for him.

8

Treed

It was cold—ten below according to the outdoor thermometer hanging on the garage door. Percy chewed a bowl of Wheaties and a slice of white Wonderbread toast as he sat quietly, alone, at the breakfast table. Last night Louise had turned away from him again when he crawled into bed beside her after his gig at The Flame. It was 1:30 a.m. He turned away, too, not that he wanted to, but that he felt obliged. She knew about Judy and him. He knew about her suitor.

In fact, it seemed everyone knew about it. Their marriage had become a topic at St. Thomas Episcopal, though opinions differed as to who was more at fault. Idle gossip aside, many parishoners knew Percy and Louise well and cared about them both. Their assessment was, "They were too young." They'd gotten married before they had time to discover how incompatible their life-styles were. Louise wanted a man with a day job who spent his evenings at home with the wife and kids or attending PTA meetings and athletic events. She wanted a husband who would mend the leaky faucet or paint the porch. Percy, on the other hand, wanted a wife who was part of his music, if not as a performer, then as an appreciative listener who rode home with him after the show, sharing his musical high, and made love 'til the wee hours of the morning.

Finishing his breakfast that morning, Percy left the house before the others awakened, wearing his woolen mail uniform, cap, and overshoes, with a red scarf wrapped securely around his neck. He closed the back door quietly and drove his 1949 Ford to the post office, where he picked up his leather mail bag. It was February 11, 1955. The bag was stuffed mostly with valentines. He would be delivering love cards to countless people, young and old, on his route that day. Some would get a dozen, others none. One widow got a valentine each year from, he discovered, her sister. He thought about her loneliness and his as he parked his mail truck on 39th and Lyndale and began his morning trek. This cold winter morning few people would be out to greet him. Those who saw him coming would open the door just long enough to reach for the mail, with a "Hi, Percy, cold enough for you?"

"Sure is, how's Arthur's back doing?"

"Better...Keep warm," and she disappeared behind a closed door.

At 3940 Lyndale the greeting was a growl from a Doberman Pincher that the owner, Don Smith, had promised to keep on a leash. On this cold day the leash was apparently too far out of reach—or else the owner didn't anticipate meeting anyone on such a morning. The fanged menace spotted Percy from three houses away and took after him. Percy had learned that running was an invitation to greater peril and stood motionless, hoping the dog would lose interest. He did, but not before he'd grabbed Percy's pant leg, pulled his legs out from under him, and bit him on the ankle deeply enough to leave the imprint of both jaws. The monster finally responded to his master's whistle and galloped homeward.

Percy considered dropping Smith's mail in the snow ten feet from their front door, but gentleman that he was, he delivered the mail as usual and resolved to write a letter to Mr. Smith, warning him politely that if the dog attacked him again, he'd report it to the pound.

When he returned to the Post Office at noon, he had the wound treated and filed a report—one of four such reports he filed over the years.

By three p.m. he'd finished his route; he drove home, read the *Minneapolis Star* until the kids returned from school, inquired about their latest adventures, and had a bite to eat. Louise prepared an excellent meal that night, in spite of spending the day at *The Spokesman*. It was a hot beef sandwich and mashed potatoes, gravy and green beans. With the children present neither Percy nor Louise said a word about the palpable tension that had developed between them. By seven he was out the door to The Flame Café. He arrived a bit early at the request of the establishment's owner and manager, Ray Perkins, who sat down across from him when he arrived.

"Percy," he smiled, " I got a great new show for you. You know my brother's show at the Gay Nineties, the male strippers? Well, I've got this act, see, with four guys cross dressing as women, dancing in high heels with stuffed tits. They call themselves the Jewel Box Revue. They're really good. In fact, they're better than some of the dancing dolls."

"You mean they're taking over my show?"

"No, no, no, I want you and your band, a smaller band, of course, to back them up, play for 'em. I mean, you got the music. You'll draw your regular customers, and the act will bring more."

"More what, Ray?"

"More clientele, more customers. That's what we're about, isn't it? You'll be playing for more people every night. You can't beat that." He paused for a moment while studying Percy's expression. "What's the matter? You look like you were just bitten by a dog."

"Make that two dogs," Percy muttered.

"Huh?"

"Nothing. So when does this new act begin?"

"Next week on Tuesday. Can you rehearse Monday evening on your day off. I'll pay you extra."

"Do I have a choice?"

"Hey, look Percy. I don't want to lose you. You and I have

done well by each other. I'm looking out for you. Jazz isn't bringing in the people the way it was when you started. It's not your fault. You have a loyal following, but the young people are going over to country and this Elvis Presley guy. I don't know what they see in it. Personally, I like your stuff best, but things change, you know.

"Okay, I'll do it...because I have to play. I play where I'm wanted."

"And you're wanted here. Make no mistake about it."

That night he told Judy and the band. Then, trying to be positive, he told his audience. It seemed the end of an era. The music scene was changing. Rock and roll, the folk revival, and country western were nudging jazz aside. The young audience had not been schooled in jazz. It seemed intellectual to them, a medium of their parents' generation. It was one of the saddest evenings of Percy's life as a band leader, a real two dog day. When Judy sang, "It don't mean a thing if it ain't got that swing," it took on a whole new meaning. Tomorrow he would send valentines to III and Cheryl and buy a box of chocolates in a heart-shaped box for Louise. This, too, was about surviving.

Percy's reduced back-up group for the Jewel Box Revue now consisted of Marv Dahlgren on drums, Stan Haugesag on trombone, Percy on alto, Jack Kryzinski on guitar, and Howard Williams on bass. But playing backup for the bump and grind of a male stripper routine didn't sit well with Percy—he found it seamy and embarrassing—and he began to dream immediately of escaping to play his own music again. He was still able to arrange real swing and bebop gigs occasionally, in an effort to maintain his dignity. But when Larry Hork, a downtown restauranteur, sent one of his bartenders to The Flame one night in 1956, Percy was eager to listen to his offer.

At intermission, Guy Mortenson approached Percy and asked for a moment of his time. Percy mumbled something to Howard Williams about this man who wanted to talk to him about a job. Had Percy been satisfied where he was, he would have said so and dismissed the invitation. But any job offer now was intriguing.

"You know Larry Hork?" Mortenson inquired.

"I've met him. I've been to his restaurant. We talked a little," Percy replied leaning into the conversation.

"Well, Harry is opening a new place out in Golden Valley straight west on Olson Highway. It's where the highway and Country Club Road meet. It'll be called The Point."

"Well, I don't know. What's he offering?"

"It'll be a dinner and dance club with your band as the mainstay five nights a week."

"Do I get to play my music?"

"Absolutely. That's what he wants--good jazz and swing the way you play it. . . and Judy Perkins."

This was too good to be true. Within fifteen minutes he had worked out the contract details and scheduled an interview with Larry Hork. He wanted to meet the man for whom he'd be working before he'd sign on. But the prospect sounded inviting. He'd have his quartet and Judy five nights a week offering up jazz, jazz, jazz and the best dance music in town. He and his band had reached the end of a dismal two years. Now he would be a true band leader again at The Point Supper Club. The Point. He liked the sound of it.

9

"I'm In Another World"

The Point

World War II had been over for nearly eight years and the Korean armistice was about to be signed when Dennis Scholtes, listening outside the stage door of the Flame Café, accepted the invitation to come inside and enjoy Percy Hughes and his Orchestra from backstage. The Cold War was underway and the rampant accusations of Senator Joe McCarthy were destroying the lives of hundreds of innocent Americans at the time, but Scholtes was focused on living the life of a dance band musician. He traveled the countryside with the Amby Meyer Band from the Surf Club in Clear Lake, Iowa, to the Cobblestone in Storm Lake, then on to the Roof Garden in Okeboji, the Interlachen in Fairmont, Minnesota, the Turp in Austin, and the Kato in Mankato. Enthusiasts were still filling the dance halls throughout the Midwest, and his was only one of many territory bands covering the region. Scholtes followed his dream to MacPhail Music School in Minneapolis and in 1958 joined Jules Herman, the house band at the Prom Ballroom in St. Paul.

But the music scene was changing along with the mood of the nation. In 1955 Elvis Presley rocked the nation with his brand of country blues rock and transformed the pop scene forever. While Frank Sinatra, Perry Como, Bobby Darin, Ella Fitzgerald and even a young Andy Williams remained popular, the young had found a new hero, leaving behind the songs of Hoagy Carmichael, Johnny Mercer, and Cole Porter for "Heartbreak Hotel" and "Jailhouse Rock." They dropped the Lindy and other popular dance hall routines and took up the twist. They cavorted at sock hops in high school gymnasiums to "Rock Around the Clock" and "Blue Suede Shoes."

A few years later, The Kingston Trio introduced a commercial brand of folk music, scoring a hit with a recording of "Tom Dooley." Other similarly smooth vocal groups soon became equally popular on college campuses, including the Brothers Four, The Limelighters, and Peter, Paul and Mary; and the crusty originals who had kept the folk traditions alive began to attract more attention themselves, Pete Seeger perhaps foremost among them. Newcomers such as Bob Dylan, Joan Baez, and Arlo Guthrie (following in father Woody's footsteps) emerged on the scene, and by the time the surfing craze and the British Invasion were in full swing, the nation's taste for Big Band music was in serious decline. Dance halls were closing right and left, and the bands that were left were changing their tone and migrating to supper clubs.

Since blacks were not invited to play in the ballrooms, Percy was never a part of that scene. Folks danced to his music, but in the night clubs where he performed the guests dined and listened as well. Percy never lost his love of the music of Jay McCann and Johnny Hodges, or the great bands of Duke Ellington and Count Basie, which continued to tour the country, but by the time he arrived at The Point in 1956, the transformation was underway. Many listeners wanted something else.

Percy opened at The Point on Olson Highway and Winnetka in Golden Valley with a jazz quartet that included Tom Slobodzian at piano, Howard Williams on bass, Jack Bertleson on drums, Percy himself on reeds, and Judy Perkins at the mike. The group played five nights a week, drawing jazz aficionados from around the Twin Cities metro area. Some locals considered the cars in the parking lot and the largely-urban clientele to be a nuisance. But since the establishment sat across from city hall and the fire and police departments, the authorities were fully prepared to handle inappropriate behavior. And little of such behavior occurred. Some of the guests came for good food, others for the jazz. In the smoky atmosphere the mood shifted with the music. Judy Perkins's rich voice glided over the notes of "Don't Get Around Much Anymore," "Just You, Just Me," and "See What Happens" with such feeling that listeners often dropped their conversation and followed every nuance. Percy's tenor sax further enchanted the performance with coloration and depth. Local critics and media commentators Cedric Adams, Will Jones, and Don Morrison, were in agreement that these performers were top notch, and in their columns they frequently reminded readers of the musical treasures to be found just west of the city.

Leigh Kamman

As usual, Leigh Kamman stood foremost among Percy's local promoters. In 1956 he had just returned from a six-year engagement in New York. He and his vocalist wife, Patti McGovern, had moved there to pursue their respective careers; she had joined a progressive quintet called the Honey Dreamers, and after leaving that group she recorded an album, *Wednesday's Child*, with arranger Thomas Talbert (also from Minnesota) which many devotees of the art of jazz vocal recording still consider a landmark in the field. Leigh, meanwhile, worked at WOV radio as a broadcaster and interviewer at the Palm a few blocks from the Apollo Club on a show called, "Life Begins at Midnight" that aired throughout New England and on the ships at sea from 8 p.m. until 3 a.m. every night. There he interviewed the New York jazz musicians and entertainers such as Ellington, Cab Calloway, Sidney Portier, and Harry Bellefonte. His radio partner was one Diane Johnson, who later took the name Diahann Carroll and became a Broadway and television star. When he returned to Minneapolis, Leigh soon hooked up with WLOL, which gave him an afternoon show. He later moved to KSTP. In pointing out jazz venues he often promoted The Point as the place to go to hear the finest jazz around.

A patron entering The Point on an early evening in the late 1950s might have seen a few people seated at the bar who had stopped in for a drink before heading to homes in Plymouth, Loretto, or Rockford. Irv Fischer would be standing behind the bar taking orders. Straight ahead the new arrival would see the doors to the dining room where Chef DeCamboliza prepared the meals. Dinner guests who would begin to trickle in at about 6 p.m. to be seated at tables set with white linen tablecloths. Many of them would enjoy a high-ball or Manhattan, order a top sirloin or t-bone steak, and wait for the arrival of Percy and his quartet, to whose music they would later dance the evening away. Many of these guests were from the Isles and Kenwood area, which was hardly more than ten minutes away, though the club was also popular with professionals from nearby Tyrol Hills, Minnetonka, Wayzata, and St. Louis Park. For those who wanted a somewhat lighter meal and some good music in a quieter venue, the upstairs piano bar might be featuring virtuoso jazz guitarist Reuben Ristrom.

This was the way it was at The Point for seventeen years. The Hughes band would open with Percy's theme song, "Satin Doll," an Ellington favorite, placing the music before him as if he still needed it after having played it hundreds of times. That ritual was a matter of style rather than need. Then he'd count: one, two, a one, two three four at a moderate tempo that

Percy's band in March 1966 showed a few younger faces. From left—Joel Beale, Tom Slobodzian, Percy Hughes, Bruce Calin. Judy Perkins joined the group on Saturday nights.

characterized many of his numbers. Reuben Ristrom pointed out that when Percy was really charged up he'd say, "Okay, let's burn one" and begin with the same count in the same tempo. It didn't matter. Every tune was played with style and passion.

Of course, the decor, the menu, and the musicians in the band at the Point changed from time to time. By 1972 the Peterson brothers, Billy and Bob, played bass and piano, respectively while Joe Beale finessed the drumset. And Carol Martin replaced Judy Perkins as vocalist when she took her solo act downtown to places like the Golliwog at the Sheraton Ritz. In early '73 the Hughes band made a recording featuring Carol Martin in an album co-produced by Leigh Kamman and Dick Driscoll entitled "Live at the Point" with Percy on reeds, Tom Slobozian on piano, Bruce Calin on bass, Joe Beale on drums. The album is archived at the Minnesota Historical Society for those who might want to hear Carol sing,, "I Want to Shout," "The Look of Love," "Hallelujah, I Love Him So," "Chicago" and "Going Out of My Head" backed up by the band.

Meanwhile, having always thought of herself as a nightclub singer for dancing couples, Judy Perkins now reprogrammed herself to be a performer. She had never thought of herself as the main attraction, but simply part of the band delivering dance music.

She had begun her career in an Omaha, Nebraska, night club with her sister, who later led an all-girl jazz group called "Sweethearts of Rhythm." As a young woman she'd aspired to become a doctor, but one thing led to another and she eventually found her way to Minneapolis, where she met Percy. He recognized her talent and hired her. She'd intended to take singing lessons, too, but that never happened, and according to many, never needed to. Judy had a natural gift, and after years of experience in front of the mike, she'd become adept at interpreting a song.

While Percy's long-term bookings at the Flame Café and The Point fulfilled his need to make music, it did nothing to improve his relations at home with Louise, and in 1959 the couple agreed it was time to divorce. Percy III was 16 at the time and Cheryl was ten. From that point on, Percy no longer came home in late afternoon after finishing his mail route to greet his children. He no longer sat at the dining room table with the family, sharing the day's events before he left for a gig. He took the children fishing from time to time and saw them at church, but it was Judy Perkins sitting beside him in the pew, not Louise.

That romance had been kindled the day she began singing with his orchestra at the Treasure Inn, and it grew warmer during their early years at The Flame Café. For twelve of their fourteen years together they were a happy couple. They were living their loves--music and each other.

79

Percy's long run at The Point came to an abrupt end on October 18, 1973. A friend called Percy at home that afternoon asking him if he'd left his instruments at the club. "On the bandstand," he said, "where I always leave them. Why?"

"The Point is on fire!" the friend exclaimed. Percy hurried to the scene. To his relief, the fire had started upstairs and

firefighters had been brought it under control before it reaching the bandstand. Percy packed his alto, tenor, and clarinet, and then watched as firemen poured water on the place where he had worked for years. It was a cold day. He noticed a reporter from the *Golden Valley Sun* interviewing a bartender. Firelight flickered across the faces of bystanders, and also, it seemed, across the years of wonderful music that had been generated here, which would remain alive in the memories of the devotees who'd come night after night to hear fine jazz.

When the Point eventually reopened, Percy Hughes was no longer on the bill. He was pleased when Oscar Husby, owner of the Ambassador Motor Lodge in nearby St. Louis Park, invited him to play at the lodge's supper club, The Kashmiri Room, a plush place with a small dance floor ideal for dress-up dinner romancing.

In that same year Judy became ill. At first she was diagnosed with a thyroid condition. When treatment failed, her physician told her she had cancer. It was too late by then to do anything much. For weeks Percy spent as much time with her as he could and in the last days seldom left her side. He watched as his love slipped off into the night a year later on New Year's Eve 1974.

Now he was alone. With little time to recover from Judy's death, he had to face the fading health of his father, with whom he had spent so many hours reeling in pan fish on Fish Lake. In spite of the heartache and loneliness, Percy dutifully packed up his horns and drove to his gigs four nights a week at the Kashmiri Room.

For nine years an appreciative audience listened to Percy and his trio, which also included an organ and a guitar. Dean Holmes was the organist for two years before Nancy Lovgren took his place. Joe Rucci was a mainstay on guitar, though he, too, was eventually succeeded by Bob Caldwell.

When Percy first accepted Husby's invitation to join Dean Holmes at the Ambassador, Nancy Lovgren was playing with Joe Rucci at a strip club in downtown Minneapolis near the Gay Nineties. Rucci had played with Percy at The Point and he joined him at the Ambassador. When Dean Holmes left as the organist, Joe invited Nancy to audition. She had admired Percy from a distance since she was seventeen years old and approached the audition with both anticipation and trepidation. When she learned that Tommy Bower, an esteemed pianist, had also auditioned, she suspected that her try-out was in vain. The next day, however, she got the call from Percy inviting her to be his organist. Dumbfounded, she accepted, and continued to play with Percy in many venues until recently.

The music that the trio was expected to play in the Kashmiri Room was different from what Percy enjoyed playing most. Percy continued to play jazz as often as he could sneak it in, but Oscar preferred "easy listening" numbers on the order of "Josephine" and "Sentimental Journey." Quiet, subdued numbers for dining were interspersed with instrumental versions of pop standards on the order of "Moon River" and "The Shadow of Your Smile." But owner Oscar Husby also loved Scandinavian music, and Percy learned to sing "Helsa Dem Där Hemma" in fractured Swedish to accommodate his taste. Somehow to the audience it didn't seem incongruous that a handsome black jazzman was singing Swedish in a dining club.

One night Nancy Lovgren remembers Percy's mother, Virginia, and his brother, Clayton, dancing the night away to numbers such as "Alley Cat." Nothing made Percy happier than watching them dance to his music. He enjoyed giving back to them what he could. That night he snuck in "Poor Butterfly" in memory of the duets he and Clayton played together in their youth upon his mother's request.

The audience loved Percy. They doted on him. His friends adored him no matter what he played. "He has a charisma," Nancy said, "that draws people to him. It's his musicianship, certainly, but more than that—it's personality. Of course, it doesn't hurt that he's handsome." When people approached him during intermission, they experienced his generous spirit. "He made them feel good," she said. Whatever else was going on in their lives seemed unimportant at that moment. Intermission was request time and the newer crowd, learning that Percy was approachable, most often requested "something peppy."

Imagine, if you will, the posh Kashmiri Room, on the lower level of a suburban motor hotel, with white linen table clothes, elegant scarlet draperies, crystal glassware, soft lighting, bouquets on the tables, cushioned velvet chairs, plush carpet, and guests chatting over a glass of wine as they look forward to a gourmet meal and a night of the Percy Hughes trio. Imagine, too, the trio's ascent from the lower level with their instruments via the elevator, a cubicle in an ugly shaft that dropped to collected water on the basement floor. Behind the posh accoutrements and presentation lay the deteriorating substructure so familiar to the staff. The place was all about appearances. Everything was offered to please the public--the best food and the most talented musicians playing, if not the best music, then the music the audience most wanted to hear.

Percy, Nancy Lovgren, and Bob Caldwell at the Kashmiri Room

It was a good gig, but as far as Percy was concerned, it wasn't the Flame Room or even The Point. The trio played the prescribed selections, jazzing them up from time to time to expand the musical taste of their audience.

Another continuing source of distress to Percy were the remarks he'd occasionally pick up from employees and guests that carried racist overtones. Nor was such discrimination reserved for blacks. Nancy also suffered the condescension of listeners who were unaccustomed to see a female instrumentalist on stage. Nancy would occasionally receive such backhanded compliments as, "You play pretty well for a woman." And any mistake she happened to make was not only professionally embarrassing, it also reinforced the stereotype of women's natural inferiority. When she did make a mistake, a seldom occurrence, she avoided Percy's eyes, thinking that surely he countenanced a scornful expression. She assumed he was as demanding of her as he was of himself. But Percy admired her work and told her often. He, too, made mistakes, though the audience seldom noticed them. Still, after one performance Nancy, feeling woefully inadequate, presented Percy with a large plastic ear so that he would be sure not to miss the next errant note. He chuckled and said something like "I only hear your music."

It's true, Percy expected perfection of himself. One night he apologized to the audience for a mistake he made, after which Nancy pointed out that the apology was more embarrassing than the mistake. Percy understood and never apologized for a musical error again. Their mistakes were few, however, and their relationship a musical delight. Nancy was better grounded in the pop material and provided strong support for Percy when he was forced outside of his comfort zone. And fans from the big band days who had attended the shows at the Flame and The Point continued to enjoy Percy's warm, lyrical sound at the Kashmiri Room. Over the years he had become an icon for jazz lovers.

10

"Day Dream"

From Loss to New Love

While Percy enjoyed steady work at the Ambassador, he was lonely. He continued his postal route and organized golf and tennis events during the day, but came home to an empty house. He didn't know he was about to meet the woman whom he would love for the rest of his life.

Dolores Violette, called Dee, was born with a deformation of both feet that forced her to walk on her insteps. In spite of her labored and clumsy gait, she maintained a positive outlook and prepared herself for her future. She married and raised five children. Soon, however, she discovered that the man she married had debilitating emotional problems that left him unable to work for 17 of the 24 years they were married. Once again making the best of a bad situation, Dolores worked full time, cared for her children and managed the household on her own. The husband's drinking problems finally grew so unmanageable that she divorced him in 1973.

In the same year, she had surgery on her left foot, removing intrusive bones and adding artificial toes. For the first time she could walk with only a minor limp.

Shortly after her divorce, and with two children still in high school, she took a job with Med-care Associates, a company that leased and operated three nursing homes. As an administrative assistant at their Westwood facility, her main function was to become thoroughly schooled in the ever-changing laws regarding reimbursement from Medicare and Medicaid and to assure that Westwood received all the funds to which it was entitled. (She had held a similar job during the 1950's supervising Medicare reimbursements.) At the time she lacked a nursing license, but passed the required test and became a licensed practical nurse. In time Dee became an expert in regulations, forms, applications and procedures of county, state, and nation.

As a result of her growing expertise, Med-care Associates assigned her to monitor payments at their other nursing homes. When she succeeded in filling all of Westwood's 200 beds, she and the staff decided to have a celebration. She mentioned her interest in having music for the event to Rufus Webster, a man who often visited his mother-in-law at the Westwood Home. Rufus was a pianist. In fact, he'd played at The Flame with Percy. Rufus said he could get the best band in town for her, and called his old friend Percy, who organized six pieces to play gratis for the occasion. The band played for an hour such tunes as "Time After Time," "Blue Skies," "Hello Dolly," and "Autumn Leaves" to great applause. The demand for encores extended the show for another half hour.

Dee had known and admired Percy's work for a long time. She'd been listening to it since his early days at the Calhoun Beach Club and Radisson Hotels, and had followed his career at Treasure Inn, the Flame Café, and the Point. She'd listened to Leigh Kamman's interviews with him on MPR and *The Jazz Image*. But she had never met Percy, until now.

During the performance Percy noticed an attractive woman mingling with the residents, her eyes aglow and smiling. She moved from one to another, engaging them in bits of conversation and making sure they were comfortable. As the members of the band seated themselves with the residents for lunch, Percy approached her and said, "I've been watching you. You seem to love everybody in this room. Do you work here? You kind of fascinate me."

Taken aback by this gentle but candid approach, she muttered, "Why, yes, I do. I'm the residence administrator."

"I thought you must be important," Percy smiled. "Would you like to have dinner with me sometime?"

Dolores raced through her commitments and responsibilities while continuing her appraisal of this man. During his playing she had been enamored with both his musicianship (of which she was already well aware) and his demeanor. She sensed his kindness from the moment he entered the room.

After a moment of silence she smiled and said, "That would be nice." At the time she'd been divorced for three years, but had not been seriously pursuing a new relationship. But there was something about him.

The next day, Monday, he called, having rummaged through the pages of the phone book for Westwood Nursing Home. When the receptionist answered, he said, "I'd like to speak to the administrator whom they call Dee. This is Percy Hughes."

"Dee," she called, "there's a Percy Hughes on the line, wants to talk to you."

"Yes?" she answered.

"Hi, Dee. I'm sorry I don't know your whole name. This is Percy Hughes. I played sax at the residence yesterday."

"Yes, of course. You invited me to dinner sometime. I'm Dolores Violette, but everybody calls me Dee.

"Hi, Dee Violette. Nice to meet you," he chuckled. "You see, there's a fish fry at Eddy Boike's home tonight. Eddie's a sax player and a good friend of mine. Would you like to go with me?"

Dee said "yes" before considering the arrangements she would have to make.

That was the beginning of a relationship that has continued for thirty-four years—so far.

At first, the two of them found it difficult to arrange times to see each other, with both of them working during the day and Percy playing at the Ambassador at night. In the course of the coffee dates they did set up, Dee got to know Percy better. She was impressed by his love for his family and his unusual willingness to talk about Judy Perkins, for whom he continued to grieve. She could tell that theirs had been a devoted love and affection, a companionship that when severed left him dazed and lost. It depressed him to eat without her. He felt as if he were sentenced to solitary confinement for a crime he hadn't committed. She thought that she might be the first person with whom he shared his grief so openly. She hadn't met a man of such honesty, a man so in touch with his emotions, and so caring.

Only a couple of weeks after they first met, Percy suggested that Dee come meet his parents at a family dinner celebrating his father's 79th birthday. The dinner was held at a restaurant in south Minneapolis. As it was nearing adjournment for dessert at the Hughes home on 5th Avenue, Clayton got up to leave.

"It's time to go," he said. Dee, however, wasn't ready to leave. She felt the conversation was still ripening into family fruit and needed the time another cup of coffee would afford. She turned toward Clayton upon his second step away from the table and suggested with false diffidence and a smile, "Let's have some more coffee." To which Percy's mother, Virginia, smiled, "I like your style."

They drank more coffee. Clearly, Virginia and Dee were compatible from the start. They had the same energy and perspective, the same assertive winsomeness. Dee would have no difficulty becoming part of the family.

During that visit Dee learned that Sr. hadn't fully recovered from a stroke a year earlier. He walked with a limp and slurred his words a bit, but he was energetic and warm. She saw how much his boys cared for him. It made her feel comfortable. She enjoyed them all.

A few days later Sr. had a heart attack and developed congestive heart failure. He was in the hospital for a time, then home in the upstairs bedroom. While Virginia was loving and provided him with excellent meals and companionship, she wasn't a caregiver. That was Dee's calling. She bathed him, cut his toenails, and trimmed his straight hair that he said he inherited from his Cherokee ancestors. She listened to him talk about his boys as if they were still children, climbing trees, playing baseball and tooting "Poor Butterfly" on their trumpet and clarinet. Dee arrived after work, often missing Percy who visited daily after his postal route, but she would see him on his nights off.

Another heart attack put Sr. back in the hospital and then back to their upstairs bedroom. One evening Percy came downstairs where Dee and Virginia were talking and took Dee's hand. "Sr. told me to marry you before he dies. Will you marry me?" He smiled with a smile no one had ever said no to.

Dee and Percy had talked about marriage but hadn't made any definite plans. They seemed to agree earlier that such an event was a year away. Now this. She loved Percy; she knew that. But she had an apartment and he had a house. She had two boys at home and they hadn't discussed the finances.

"When?" she asked, trying to process this new turn of events. They set the date for May 2. They were married at St. Thomas Episcopal Church with Clayton as best man and Father Richard Smith officiating. Seven days later, on May 9, 1977, Percy, Sr., knowing his son was married to a loving woman, died in peace.

From that moment on, when Percy attended St. Thomas Episcopal Church, Dee sat beside him. Virginia made sure of that. She demanded regular attendance. Such a demand presented no problem for Dee. She felt at home at St Thomas immediately. The Hughes family were icons of the church, having donated stained-glass windows and participated in social justice and outreach programs. To this church Percy had brought his first wife, Louise, who still attended, and his two children.

After their divorce Judy sat beside him until she was too ill to attend. Now it was Dee whom the congregation welcomed with open arms.

The family still owned the cabin on Fish Lake that Percy Sr. and Virginia had purchased back in the 1940's, and Percy and Dee drove out there to relax as often as they could. Clayton later parked his motor home on the property permanently beside the quaint cabin and he and his family lived there. But the newlyweds wanted a place of their own, and in 1978 they bought a small cabin on the west side of Hwy 169 south of Garrison. They and their guests fished in a succession of ever-larger outboard Alumicraft boats. Percy loved to fish and was thrilled that Dee also enjoyed the sport.

Percy continued to play with Nancy Lovgren and Joe Rucci at the Kashmiri Room, and he also began to do some vocals. He had a hard time remembering lyrics, however, so he'd take Dee out in the middle of Lake Mille Lacs and sing to her. Her choice

Percy, Percy III, and Percy's brother Clayton

was to listen or swim to shore. She chose to listen, coaching him with the words to "The Shadow of Your Smile," "There Will Never Be Another You," and other songs. She liked to hear him sing. He had an easy, soothing tenor voice, the kind that makes you want to cuddle up by the fire as in "You'd Be So Nice to Come Home To."

Suddenly, a tug on the line interrupted his song. Pole in hand, Dee stared at the water, waited until the fish had sucked on the juicy shiner long enough, then set the hook and pulled in a three-pound walleye. Percy took charge of the net.

When in 1982 Percy retired from the post office, the couple devoted more time for fishing.

By 1986, Dee's brother Bill was struggling with kidney cancer. During his illness, Bill and his wife Patti spent time at the lake with the Hughes. But Bill, though he loved to fish, couldn't tolerate the rough water of Mille Lacs, and Percy grew to dislike it, too. He was struggling with hip pain, and would have hip-replacement surgery three times over the next few years. The Hughes finally sold their Mille Lacs place and bought a trailer home on the much smaller (and calmer) Farm Island Lake between Garrison and Aiken. There the four could fish in relative comfort, pulling in lots of bass, crappies, sunfish, and even walleyes. It was Bill's final summer of camaraderie and fishing. He passed away of renal cancer in North Memorial Hospital in Robbinsdale just before Christmas, with his sister at his side.

When Percy wasn't fishing, he played a few gigs at Phil's Myr Mar Marina on the west side of Mille Lacs Lake, or traveled a few miles to Aiken where he gave tennis lessons on the municipal courts for the city recreation program. A tennis player from his youth, he developed coaching skills that made him one of the best coaches of seniors in the country.

After Percy and Dee married in 1977, they consolidated by buying a condo in St. Louis Park at 7313 West Franklin so that Dee's two sons could continue at St. Louis Park High School.

Percy and Dee

Percy sold his home at 4401 Clinton Avenue South, where he had lived with Judy, and moved in with Dee. The couple lived there for fourteen years before moving in 1991 to a home around the corner in the same complex with a two car garage at 2034 Louisiana.

The gig at the Kashmiri Room ended in 1982, at which point the trio (with Bob Caldwell now on guitar) accepted a running engagement at the Bel Aire Yacht Club. But the sound system garbled their music and the crowd preferred "corny" stuff to jazz; that gig didn't last long, mostly by the band's choice. From then on, Percy and his cohorts were itinerant.

During this time Percy finally got to work on a project that had been in the back of his mind for some time—cutting an album to pay special tribute to Judy Perkins. "We had planned to do an album together, but when she knew she wasn't going to make it, she ordered me to do the album and to do the singing in her place," Percy sighed. He even took more singing lessons at MacPhail to be worthy of singing her songs. From the time Dee first met Percy, she could feel his deep love for Judy, and she also encouraged Percy to cut a record in her honor.

The final impetus to proceed with the recording project was Percy's declining health. He had struggled with lung congestion from what was apparently a cold or bronchitis. Several doctors suggested that he let the malady take its course, but the congestion didn't leave him. One afternoon in July in 1982, he was playing a hot match with Dr. Nixon, a good friend, when his on-court adversary noticed that Percy was struggling for breath. Upon further examination, Nixon ordered Percy to the hospital, where he was treated for viral pneumonia and a collapsed lung.

For some time he had struggled with phrasing the tunes the way he used to. Now he knew why. He was losing his breath capacity. Would he ever have the lung power again? Before his lungs got even worse he would have to make the album for Judy. Dee was right. It was now or never.

The next year Percy entered the studio to record *I Remember Judy* under the direction of sound engineer Miles Wilkinson. Leigh Kamman was production manager, and Percy was joined by Reuben Ristrom on guitar, Dick Norling on bass, Red Wolfe on trumpet, and Dick Bortolussi on drum. Wilkinson and Gordy Knutson had set up a sound studio in the Knutson basement. The lead song on the album was a live 1965 recording of Judy singing "Mac the Knife." The remaining songs,

I Remember Judy

Percy Hughes with the Red Wolfe Quartet

sung by Percy, were some of Judy's favorites, including "Satin Doll," "Don't Get Around Much Anymore," "Every time You Touch Me I Get High," "Just Me, Just You," "Blues for Judy,"

"Just Squeeze Me," "Watch What Happens," "Red Top," "Come in From the Rain," and "Perdido." Dick Bortolussi recalled that the recording event was very emotional. "Percy seemed to be pouring out his heart to Judy through his sax. He sang her songs to her as if he were holding her hand and looking into her eyes." The album release party was held at the Brandywine Nightclub in New Brighton; Percy played that night with the Red Wolfe band.

In a recent interview Nancy Lovgren recalled other fine musicians who played with Percy. Drummer Dick La Vay began playing with Percy at The Point at age 14, subbing for Jack Bertleson, and often played with him later. Paul Mazzacano, another fine drummer, played with Percy off and on. The group played at a tennis banquet, at the Chart House in Lakeville, and several other places around town. Nancy noted how nervous Percy was the first time they played together at St. Thomas Episcopal. Perhaps he felt like the little boy just learning the clarinet standing beside his brother playing the trumpet to Christmas carols. But then Percy was often nervous about arrangement. He wanted everything right.

At a black venue—she couldn't remember where—Nancy met Louise, Percy's first wife, whom she described as warm and friendly. She also recalled how Percy had described the abuse that Judy Perkins suffered in her first marriage. Judy had a daughter from that marriage. Sadly, after Judy's death Percy was unable to maintain a relationship with her. Judy's loss drove him into depression to the point of contemplating suicide. Nancy spoke of the performance for the Westwood Nursing Home when he met Dolores Violette. She commented, "Dee came up to Jack Bertleson, a handsome man, and said, 'You look just like my husband.' to which he responded, 'Was he wonderful?' and her response, "Well, let's just say he had some issues."

Jack, who drummed for Percy many times over the years, became a close friend. More than once he shoveled Percy's sidewalk while Percy walked his postal route. All the musicians who played with Percy cared for him, because he cared for them. He always gave credit to his sidemen, the other players in the band, and he always paid them union scale.

As a Democrat of conviction, Percy had trouble playing for conservative groups. At one gathering he observed several blacks among the Republican audience. It infuriated him to think a black man or woman could belong to a party that discounted black people in life and law. When the gig was over, he left immediately, sputtering and muttering.

At one gig at the IDS Center the band entertained a gathering of black professionals. Percy's trio played "Sweet Georgia Brown" while members of the audience performed a superb line dance that left the band members in awe. The trio also played for the American Legion Club, the Postal Workers, Minnesota Mining Black Days and many other organizations.

11

Big Band Revival

Rendezvous with Rhythm

During his last years at The Point and his nine years at the Kashmiri Room at the Ambassador, Percy worked to bring jazz to colleges and universities as a legitimate subject for study. He became close friends with Dr. Reginald Buckner, pianist and associate professor of African American Studies at the University of Minnesota. Through Reginald, Percy became a music educator.

"What matters most is what's in here." Percy pointed to his heart as he stood in front of Reginald's Afro-American Studies students in Scott Hall on the University of Minnesota campus. "That's where music comes from. Of course, the musician must know the tune, know the musical patterns of the song, and play around with it, but he must always feel where it wants to go. You know your instrument, you know the tune, you play from the heart."

With that, he hooked his alto sax to his neck strap, looked over at Reginald Buchner seated at the piano nearby, and brought up "Tenderly" to live again. The students listened intently—mesmerized, in fact.

It was 1970. The course, "Music of Black America," was being offered a second time, and once again Percy was among the many guests Bruckner had brought in to share their experience and musicianship with young students learning about the

96

heritage of jazz. As Percy answered questions about his youth and early career, and the musicians who had influenced him—Duke Ellington, Jay McShann, and Johnny Hodges, among many others—he noticed Doris Hines, a fine jazz singer, in the audience. Doris, in order to learn more about her heritage, had begun taking classes in Afro-American studies. When Percy saw her, he asked her to come up and sing one of her favorite numbers, "Satin Doll." She didn't need to be asked twice.

A few years later, in 1976, he said to Lillian Warren, reporter and columnist for *The Spokesman*, "Music is my love...I would like to share what I know with students. Maybe they will be the ones to bring fine music back." He realized that although jazz forms continued to evolve, with "funk" and "fusion" being its newest off-shoots, the style of music he loved—swing—was slipping into the past. Yet Percy believed that good music never dies. It may lie beneath the surface for a time, but then it rises again.

Percy traveled from classroom to classroom at the University and at smaller colleges throughout the state to teach young people the variety and richness of black music. He also volunteered his services to COMPAS, an arts program in the schools that allowed young people to gain from the experience, skill, and wisdom of artists in their field. They learned of the hardships, the discrimination, and the employment difficulties that black artists faced, but emphasis was placed on the joy that comes when musicians and their audience connect, when couples dance to the rhythms, and when candlelight romancing develops to the glowing tones and intricate improvisational patterns of instruments and voices.

On Feb. 4, 1977, Percy joined Reginald Buckner on piano, Jeff Groethe on bass, and Joe Pulice on percussion in a concert at the University of Minnesota School of Music in Scott Hall Auditorium. Students swarmed that winter afternoon into the august building near the Mississippi where Vern Sutton, superb tenor and voice instructor; Dr. Frank Bencriscutto of marching band fame; Dominic Argento, Pulitzer-Prize-winning composer; Phillip Brunelle, choral maestro of the Plymouth Music Series (now Vocal Essence); and famed musicologist, Johannes Reidel were on the faculty. The students took their seats, the lights went down, and from darkness rose the music.

Groups led by Reggie Buckner, Irv Williams, Percy Hughes, and Morris Wilson all played for the 3M Black History Month series in Februaty 1984. Here they ham it up together for a promotional photo.

This *ad hoc* "Big Band Sound of the 30s" played at Coffman Union in 1977.

By some accounts, Percy was the most popular of the guests who appeared in Buckner's classes. His sincerity, charm, musicianship, and enthusiasm for his craft made him a natural teacher. And Percy discovered that he enjoyed teaching as much as playing, perhaps because his love for people came through just as strongly in the classroom as in the nightclub.

That same year, 1977, was a big one for Big Band music in the Twin Cities, due largely to the efforts of Reginald Buckner and Leigh Kamman. On Feb. 13, a couple of weeks after his Scott Hall performance, Percy joined Irv Williams in a new fifteen-piece band, the "Big Band Sound of the 30's," that played at Coffman Union. The show was sponsored by the Minneapolis Musicians Union and the Afro-American Studies Department. Many of the band-members had played with Percy before at one time or another, and the event was like a big reunion, with Irv Williams, Dave Goodlow, Jimmy Hamilton, Reginald Buckner, and Ervin "Red" Wolfe on the bandstand together. Wolfe, a jazz virtuoso on trumpet, would soon found the Echoes of Ellington Band. Roberta Davis and Jim Bowman sang for the event.

The band performed again on July 6 at Northrup Plaza on the U campus. They played the music of Ellington, Andy Kirk, Jimmy Lunceford, and Count Basie. Irv and Percy soloed on saxes; Red Wolfe and Mel Carter, on trumpet; and Jerry Mullaney trombone. Roberta Davis opted out of the July event due to a scheduling conflict: she was slated for the Playboy Club on Lake Geneva that day.

Through such performances, both Percy and Irv worked to revive an appreciation for jazz among college students, many of whom were losing touch with the tradition. They wanted young music-lovers, both black and white, to appreciate the richness of their heritage, and even, perhaps, to keep it alive as musicians and fans. Bob Protzman of the *St. Paul Pioneer Press* quoted Irv Williams, "Speaking of some of the early black big bands, 'Their music has been totally neglected, especially Lunceford, I like his band even better than Duke's. It was the hardest swinging band I ever heard--precise, original. It's just a shame it's been shunted aside. To show the impact the band must have had then, people shout and clap now when we play his things."

That same winter Percy formed the Percy Hughes Swingtet with Buzzy Peterson on trumpet and valve trombone, Welton Barnett on guitar, Jimmy Hamilton on piano, Steve Barnett on bass, Red Maddock, on drums and Barbara Joyce vocalist. *The Spokesman* reported on March 31, 1977 that on March 20, the sextet had played at the Grand Portage Room of the Registry Hotel to the largest crowd ever assembled there for a musical event. They also performed on April 3 for a return engagement, "The Jazz Side of Swing." In response to the event, Ed A. Harrington, Executive Vice President of the Registry Hotel, wrote in a letter to the organizers of the event, "From the response in numbers and enthusiasm, I would say that it was a tremendous success. I do hope that you will continue such a program...Percy Hughes is a fine musician and a very highly regarded man in our community. He has a host of friends who really appreciate his character as well as his music."

12

Man About Town

Ever since Ellie Moore first proposed that Percy become a model for her agency at a Flame Café performance in 1953, Percy frequented her studio on 17th Avenue and Lake Street. Sometimes the photography took place before carefully designed sets. At other times the photo entourage would travel to a location for the right ambiance, lighting, and setting. Soon Percy's image appeared all over town. Even into his sixties Percy was in demand. In 1982 he posed in tuxedo as a pianist at a grand piano accompanying a sleek woman in a black evening gown for a Donaldson's advertisement on the back of the Guthrie playbill. His image passed down the streets of Minneapolis on the side of a city bus advertising the transit system. In 1985 he graced the Norwest Bank brochure.

In 1986, while taking a flight to Los Angeles, Dee was reading a *Better Homes and Gardens* magazine she bought off the airport stand. As she paged through, she noticed Percy posing with a family, all actors, for an article about interfering grandparents. When she asked Percy about it, he was as surprised as she.

Percy was the poster boy on a large ad for Main Jazz at the Jazz Festival, and in 1986 he appeared on the poster for a jazz festival in Richmond, Virginia called "Hot and Steaming." Target and Best Buy used him. One of his more memorable appearances was on a poster for the Metro Council of Regional

Arts in which he hung by the collar with his instruments against a white backdrop. The caption read, "Not all art is hanging in museums. Enjoy all the arts."

By the 1980's many people recognized Percy by sight, though they had no idea who he was, and would never have guessed he was a jazz musician. No one would deny he was photogenic.

For these many public displays, Percy received upfront money but no royalties. He had an offer in the late 1970s to do a national advertisement for Toro that would have brought in some real cash, but it didn't work out. The week of the shooting it rained every day, and the ad crew had to reschedule several times. When the weather finally cleared, Percy was faced with the options of calling in sick to the post office or losing the photo op. Rather than miss work on false pretenses he turned down the opportunity. "It was only money," he said.

When Percy and Dee were looking for a condo in Edinborough in Edina in 1996, Dee paged through the company advertising brochure and saw her husband posing with a family as a satisfied owner. Since then, Percy and Dee have been surprised several times to see Percy's image in a new context. They recently came upon it in a publication put out by the federal government: "Section 5 Planning Ahead," Medicare and You 2010.

13

Family

"Love's In My Heart"

From 1946, when he started his band with a handful of players from Wold Chamberlain Naval Base, to the day he retired from the post office in 1982, Percy had never been without a steady job playing music. Few jazz musicians in the Twin Cities could say the same. Having played two-and-a-half years at the Treasure Inn, six years at the Flame Café, seventeen years at The Point, and nine years at the Kashmiri Room in the Ambassador Motor Lodge, he was a mainstay in the music world, the most widely recognized and admired band leader in the Twin Cities. In addition to those steady gigs, he joined big band performances at the University of Minnesota and organized trios, quartets, sextets, and, octets that included some of the finest musicisans in the business. No patron ever left a performance scoffing at the bass player or the drummer or the other guy on reeds. Percy's groups played to consistent acclaim for weddings, anniversaries, college dances and homecoming events, and outdoor jazz concerts.

All the while he was offering his music four or five nights a week, Percy also worked from 7 a.m. to 3 p.m. delivering mail from the post office on 54th and Nicollet Avenue South. During his tenure he received awards for both attendance and customer satisfaction. He also organized tennis, soft ball, and golf leagues, set up lessons and tournaments for P.O. employees, and even initiated fishing contests on the Minneapolis lakes. In

1960 he was chair of the Minneapolis Post Office Sports Council. With the assistance of Jack Johnson at Reed Sweatt Tennis Center, he set up a post office tennis program. Percy would become a nationally recognized coach of senior players.

But through it all, family continued to play a central role in Percy's life.

When Percy and Louise divorced in 1959, their children Percy III and Cheryl chose to live with Louise. When Percy married Judy Perkins in 1961, Judy's daughter, Sandy, then thirteen, lived with her mother and stepfather for a couple of years, then moved to Iowa to live with Judy's family. The reason for the move isn't clear. Perhaps it had to do with the busy schedules of two musicians playing nightly gigs. When Judy took sick in 1973, Sandy returned to be with her mother, staying with Percy and traveling back and forth with him to the hospital. After her mother died Sandy left again for Iowa. Soon Percy learned she had married and moved away. He didn't know where. Much to his dismay, attempts to contact her failed. To this day he doesn't know where she is. "We had a good relationship," he muttered, pensively. "I wish she had kept in touch."

His son, Percy III, although troubled by his parents divorce, has followed in his father's footsteps, not as a musician but as a man of character, personality, and responsibility. Out of high school he got a job with 3M and worked his way up to be a marketer in the tapes department. He traveled extensively, capturing sales with his winsome manner and handsome smile. He married Harryette, who passed away in 2009, and gave Percy two grandchildren, Harold and Shannon, who would grow up, marry and offer Percy and Dee four great-grandchildren. In recent years Percy and Three, as he is called in the family, have enjoyed many good times, especially at the Fish Lake Cabin.

Cheryl, too, found her parent's divorce unsettling. She felt hurt and abandoned by her father's leaving, perhaps not fully understanding the circumstances. She found a good job at Honeywell where she worked for many years supporting her family.

Left to right: daughter Cheryl, Jo Jo (Cheryl's son), Harold (III's son), little Maquello (Cheryl's son), Shannon (III's daughter), Schellina (Cheryl's daughter), Steve (Cheryl's son); Percy, Louise, and Percy III are in front. Taken in 1980.

She had two children from her first relationship, Steven and Schellina, and two from her marriage to Chris Hollins. That marriage lasted seventeen years and produced JoJo and Marquello. Shortly after their separation, she became a Jehovah's Witness, a faith that has given her hope and support. Her third marriage to Chris Mabry ended in a little over a year. Her four children have given her sixteen grandchildren. Cheryl remembers that when her mother was ill, her father came to visit her every day until she died in 1994. During those visits, she believes her mother and father resolved their issues. It saddened her, however, that their time together was past.

Whenever possible Percy and Dee took their grandchildren on shopping trips for school clothes and supplies, but their busy schedules made it difficult. "I guess I wasn't a very good father," Percy bemoaned. "I was too busy working and playing to give the kids the attention they deserved. I love them all."

Most parents believe they could have done better. They recognize that naivite, inattention, and personal agendas may impede their best intentions. The best parents can hope for is that their children know they are loved, and Percy's children know that. When Percy married Dee in 1977, Dee merged her family with Percy's. She and her husband Richard had five children: Kathy, Terry, Toni, Chuck, and John. Among them they have produced eleven grandchilden and two great grandchildren.

Dee's children and grandchildren became as much a part of Percy as his own. He was especially fond of big, strapping Chuck because he was a sportsman and loved to coach little league baseball. For years Chuck taught youngsters the skills of the game at the Twin Lakes ballpark in Robbinsdale. After he died of heart failure in 1991 the ballpark was named Chuck Violette Park after him. When Percy was receiving radiation treatment for prostate cancer at North Memorial Hospital, he would stop by the ball park and muse on his stepson's life. Then he would drive to Normandale Community College to rehearse with the concert band.

Left cluster: John and Sue Violette, Russell Grant, and Jacob (John's son kneeling); Middle: Nicole (Toni's daughter), Terry, Jessica (John's daughter); Right cluster: Jenny Dee (Toni's daughter), Toni, and Josh (John's son kneeling)

14

"Pretty and the Wolf"

Sharing What You Love

During the Big Band revival led by Reginald Buckner at the University of Minnesota in the late 70's, Red Wolfe and Percy Hughes played together for the first time. While the two maestros of jazz respected each other's talent and performance, they had traveled in different circles. When Red retired from the circulation department of the *Minneapolis Star and Tribune* after twenty-two years, he devoted his time to his music. He had taken music lessons from Art Lawrence at MacPhail, the same teacher with whom Percy began his craft. He also studied with Jimmy Greco, principal trumpet with the Minneapolis Symphony. In the late 70s he had created his Port of Dixieland Jazz Band and played regularly at the Hall Brothers Emporium of Jazz in Mendota Heights. When his reed man Harry Blons took ill, Red called upon Percy to play clarinet for him.

Percy was accustomed to playing in a Johnny-Hodges style based on arrangements of Duke Ellington numbers. When Red called he said: "Red, I'm not a Dixie player."

Red retorted, "Yes, you are. You just don't know it yet. I want you in the band. The other players will do their licks first so you can listen, then you can cut loose."

"If you think so," Percy muttered, not so sure about the idea but willing to accept the challenge. So that's the way it was. Ervin "Red" Wolfe had a steady job with Port of

Red Wolfe's Ellington Echos

Dixieland Band playing twice a week at the Lower Levee Lounge in St. Paul. When Percy joined the band, he discovered that Red and Dick Norling, the bass player, had listened to and played the music of Ellington for years. Before long the three of them became close friends.

From the beginning of their association Red took interest in Percy's style. It wasn't long before Red suggested they form a band to preserve the memory of Ellington and his fine music. He didn't need to convince Percy. So in 1986 Red created the Echoes of Ellington Band with Percy and Russ Peterson on reeds, Red on trumpet, Gene Bird on trombone, Al Closmore on jazz guitar, Dick Norling on bass, Stan Hall on piano, and Dick Bortolussi on drums.

Whenever he had a spare moment, Red transcribed tunes from 78-rpm records of Ellington's music. He would listen to and record the parts of all eight pieces of the band by hand. By the time he finished this amazing project, he had developed the charts for 165 tunes. According to Stan Hall, Red was "a masterful arranger/writer."

The octet arranged a series of weekly performances on Sunday afternoons at the Hall Brothers Jazz Emporium, and in 1986, the group made a recording called "Red Wolfe's Ellington Echoes Live at the Jazz Emporium: A Jazz Repertory Ensemble." The tunes on the album were :"Hodge Podge" (written by Ellington and saxman Johnny Hodges); an Ellington medley of "Prelude to a Kiss," "Black Butterfly," and "It Shouldn't Happen to a Dream"; "The Mooch"; "What Am I Here For?"; "Rockin' In Rhythm"; "Downtown Uproar"; "Mighty Like the Blues"; "Blues On the Double"; "Mobile Bay" and "Take the A Train."

One of Red's scores.

Percy and Red had a similar passion for music, and other musicians loved to play with them. Percy himself was inspired chiefly by Ellington's work, and he was quoted by Jim Fuller of *Minneapolis Star and Tribune* (March 23, 1987) as saying that playing Ellington's music "is why I was put on this earth, my horns and Ellington's music; it's a pure love affair for me. It's like being a kid in a candy store."

Percy and Red brought the Ellington Echoes (the more popular title for the group) to many venues, including public schools and colleges, for concerts, lectures, and clinics. Both men did solo clinics, too, and each in his own way became well known for his teaching ability and popularity with students. Meanwhile, Red continued to lead the Port of Dixieland Jazz Band and Percy jobbed with his jazz quartet.

In the April 28, 1987, *St. Paul Pioneer Press-Dispatch*, Bob Protzman posted rave reviews for the Ellington Echoes at the Emporium of Jazz playing Red's new arrangement of a

Percy and Red

medley of nine of Duke's tunes that he called, "Sketches in a Du-
cal Manner." This band included Red, trumpet; Percy, alto and
clarinet; Denny Scholtes, baritone and tenor; Dave Graf, trombone; Stan Hall, piano; Al Closmore, guitar; Dick Norling, bass;
and Phil Hey, drums. Pianist Stan Hall remarked at the time on
how much fun all the musicians were having, and Protzman's
reviews suggested that the audience caught their spirit.

During the years that Percy and Red played together they
also enjoyed social outings, especially fishing together on Lake
Mille Lacs, where they were sometimes joined by other band
members. Percy said that Red became like a brother to him, and
he admired and respected Red's gentlemanly manner as much
as his musicianship. "Red offended no one," he said.

Events on college campuses, at the Emporium of Jazz, and
other clubs were bright spots in a jazz scene that was clearly
on the wane. As the number of jazz venues declined, the bands

themselves diminished to quartets and trios. Percy, along with other musicians and jazz fans in the Twin Cities, saw a need to create a clearinghouse for musicians and gigs. Acting on this perception, C. Kyle Peterson, an advertising executive in St. Paul, and Ken Green, an attorney and jazz pianist, gathered together a group of the Twin Cities most active and notable musicians in 1979 to create the Twin Cities Jazz Society. The first board of directors included Percy Hughes, Irv Williams, Syl Jones, (who became the host for the Society with "Jazz Notes" on WCAL on the St Olaf Campus), Reginald Buckner, Roberta Davis, Dr. Thomas H. Tipton, Frank Wharton, and Morris Wilson. The purpose of the organization was "to coordinate and promote bookings for local musicians." It offered a monthly newsletter that advertised upcoming gigs for jazz and thereby offered support for union musicians. Percy sat on that board for fourteen years.

The first major event sponsored by the TCJS took place at the Prom Ballroom on University Avenue on May 14, 1979, from 7 to 11:30 p.m. The All Star Jazz Showcase featured such groups as the Mouldy Figs with Reuben Ristrom and Red Wolfe, Doris Hines, the Irv Williams Quartet, Tommy O'Donnell, and the Percy Hughes Sextet, which at that time consisted of Dave Goodlow (Bass), Nancy Lovgren (piano), Pat Roberts (trumpet), Dick LaVay (drums), and Charles Andre, vocals. The Twin Cities Jazz Society is still alive and well today, and it continues to organize and promote jazz events throughout the year.

15

Retirement

Thirty-six years of steady employment in the world of music, thirty years with the postal service, family joys and sadness, the resurgence of the big band, the alliance with Red Wolfe, the intiation of the Twin Cities Jazz Society. These were all part of Percy Hughes's working years. By 1982 he was ready to retire from the post office, but not from life. In fact, his life could well serve as a model for the retirement years.

Having been retired for fourteen years myself, I can say with some confidence that retirees tend to gravitate toward one or another category of activity. Some people settle for two. A few try just about everything. Let's pretend for a moment that the categories are mutually exclusive.

The Pleasure Seekers think of their life's work as a burden from which they need relief. During their career they accepted responsibility for family needs while grabbing whatever enjoyment they could from leisure time activities and dreaming of the day the kids would leave the home, allowing them more time to pursue their personal interests. When retirement arrives, they embark on a life of leisure, maybe a second home in a gated community where they can escape from the workaday world. It's time to play.

The Explorers can't wait to learn or develop new skills, participate in innovative projects, volunteer time and talents to community service, join clubs and other social organizations, and get acquainted with people from different walks of life with whom they have had little contact during their working years.

The Tired. This group, worn out from years of work and raising family, want nothing more than to relax. They attend events on occasion but prefer to stay at home, watch television, read pulp fiction, and play cards. They gather with their kids and grandkids for special events and sometimes babysit, but only on occasion. A life of solitude suits them best.

The Hobbyists pursue a single interest they have developed over the years, which may now become a passion. The activity may be landscape painting, wood working, quilting, playing an instrument, model trains, or writing poetry or the great American novel. Some hobbyists become widely known and admired for this special interest. Others remain obscure, though it matters little to them.

The Social Activists devote most of their retired years to political and social involvement. Liberal or conservative, they preach, walk the walk, protest, write letters to their congressmen, attend committee meetings, and work hard for their causes. They spend their leisure time boning up on issues. Personal responsibilities seem like intrusions into the more important aspects of their lives.

The Spiritualist. These persons seek divine wisdom through meditation, prayer, attending retreat centers, reading the articles and books of spiritual leaders. They believe their later years are meant to bring enlightenment and serenity and devote much of their lives in finding their spiritual center.

The Hypochondriacs. No doubt retirement is an extention of a concern these people have lived with throughout their lives irrespective of their physical condition. Some have never been ill beyond the common cold or the flu, but devote a significant portion of their day reading about the latest preventatives, supplements, and medications. They spend a fourth of their income on panaceas. Some have changed their life-style because of a near death experience or a brush with a potentially fatal disease. Their goal now is to do everything right to stave off the inevitable. Though they live in hope, they are hypersensitive to life-threatening omens.

The Volunteers are other-directed people who volunteer at food shelves, take care of grandchildren, serve as aids to teachers, visit the elderly, become befrienders through their church programs, assist an elderly neighbor. They are most happy helping others feel better.

Where does Percy Hughes fall within these slightly whimsical classifications? Certainly, he is not among the Tired. Though he has always been an advocate of social justice and has participated in Democratic party politics, these activities have not commanded his full attention. While he has been a faithful Episcopalian, attending Sunday worship now at St. Nicholas Episcopal Church in Richfield, participating on committees and playing once a month for the service, these activities haven't been a preoccupation either. He has never been a hypocondriac. And while he enjoys his boat and fishing, these activities aren't the focus of his life, so one wouldn't call him a pleasure seeker. The categories into which he fits best are Hobbyist and Explorer.

After Percy retired from the post office, he devoted his attention to his interests: music, teaching, volunteering, coaching. Never did he consider changing his life style. Rather he continued to pursue what he had always loved. He led trios, quartets, sextets, and octets in many venues throughout the Twin Cities and also in the Brainard and Mille Lacs areas. With Nancy Lovgren on piano, Russ Moore on drums, and Dave Faison on bass, sometimes adding Tim Sullivan on trumpet, his quartet or quintet played for many local events. (See Appendix for list of events and venues.). Sometimes he and Nancy teamed with Carl Carlson on trumpet in a trio Carlson called The Senior All-Stars. The latter group played all around town: on the paddlewheel boats of the St. Croix and Mississippi, North Memorial Hospital, high school reunions, Jax Supper Club, Medina Ballroom, even for birthday parties and anniversaries. Still, the

Echoes of Ellington Band was his first love. It renewed both his musical career and his passion.

Another musical adventure for Percy was to join the Normandale Community College Band under the direction of Carlo Minnetti. Minnetti had heard Percy play on several occasions, starting back at his Flame Café days, and developed a friendship with him. He believed that retired professional players playing in the college band could provide good instruction in technique, practice, and style. Percy, being the educator that he is, agreed to join the band as a clarinetist. Once a man like Percy makes a commitment, he sticks to it. Eighteen years later, Percy still has a quick breakfast every Monday through Thursday, drops down to his underground garage and drives his Buick to play from nine to ten a.m. at Normandale. When James Kurschner picked up the baton from Minnetti, Percy migrated to the saxophone section and at eighty-eight continues to exercise his musical muscles.

Percy also played with the Richfield Legion Band, directed for a while by Alex Wilson, former trumpeter with the Philadephia Symphony Orchestra, and with the Westwind Concert Band in Hopkins. Although these bands did not play the musical styles he had been playing for many years, they brought back his high school band days and kept him sharp on his instruments.

16

Other Trees to Climb

Tennis

While Percy played recreational tennis occasionally during his working years, he took up the sport with more zeal after retirement. Soon he accepted an invitation from guitarist Reuben Ristrom to join a tennis foursome. At first he filled in as a sub but was soon playing regularly with Reuben, Charlie Boone of WCCO fame, and Alan Lotsberg, who had played Willy Ketchem on the kids radio program "Alex and His Dog," and was now the writer and director of a show called "Fogie's Follies."

Percy was somewhat in awe of these celebrities who treated him as an equal. But as it happens, Alan Lotsberg was also in awe of Percy. A lover of jazz, Alan had followed Percy from the time he played at The Flame Café. He had heard Judy Perkins sing on numerous occasions and was present when Percy's band backed up Sarah Vaughan. Of Percy, Alan commented, recalling a quip made by Michael Caine about Cary Grant: "'I wish I had the *savoire faire*, the poise, that he had, and then I got to meet him.' That was my feeling about meeting Percy Hughes for the first time," he said. For five years in the early '80 these celebrities forgot who they were and banged the ball back and forth every week at the Northwest Club in St. Louis Park like four kids. "I was playing with a national treasure," Percy remarked of Charlie Boone.

"Percy had an excellent ground stroke," Lotsberg said. "Since he didn't consider himself a net man, he played back most of the time."

Percy's appraisal of Lotsberg's tennis was that he "had an innate sense of anticipation. He positioned himself to meet the ball. He covered the court." However, in 1987, at the age of sixty-five, Percy had his first hip replaced, an event that ended his participation in the weekly foursome. He remembers the group with affection. They were fun-loving and boisterous to the point where neighboring players occasionally felt the need to chastise them.

Having quit the foursome, Percy started a seniors tennis club at the Northwest Club with the help of Jack Dow and Jerry Noyes. Since Percy was now offering instruction to seniors new to the game, he decided to sharpen his own skills and solicited the instruction of tennis pro Roger Boyer, a member of the USPTA (United States Professional Tennis Association). One day Percy arrived at the Reed Sweatt Tennis Center on Nicollet and 40th with a request: that he serve as a volunteer to assist Roger Boyer as a tennis instructor on the courts. That request resulted in a long time partnership and the growth over

the years of the Senior Tennis Player's Club to 2000 members, most of whom know Percy Hughes and half of whom he has instructed.

In 1984 alone Roger and Percy conducted more than 50 training clinics. During that year Percy studied for certification as a coaching pro and took the four-hour written exam in December. For the two-hour practical exam he taught a private and a group lesson, both of which were observed by Boyer. He passed on first try. Boyer claims that between 1984 and 1990, in spite of Percy's hip replacement in 1987, the two of them conducted more than 100 clinics a year all over Minneapolis in summer programs and camps.

Early morning tennis with Clayton.

In an interview on Feb. 8, 2010, Boyer said, "Percy was conscientious about teaching. He had great rapport with students. As one may say of a fine doctor, he had great bedside manner. He would start beginning seniors with twelve free lessons. By the twelfth few, if any, had decided the game wasn't for them and continued on. Unfortunately, most of them wanted to stay with Percy as their coach, but that wasn't possible since Percy had to start a new class of beginners." Boyer continued, "No matter with whom he worked, he felt compelled to see that no student felt stressed, anxious, or frustrated with his game. He found a way to keep people involved. He relieved pressure with his soothing manner. In fact, he repaired damage inflicted by others. When players left a lesson, he made sure they were feeling positive about themselves." Until recently Percy conducted the Thursday morning seniors group from nine to ten at the Reed Sweatt Center.

During lessons, Coaches Roger and Percy prepared the court with a ball machine to fire the missiles across the net to the student player. Several times Percy set up the target on the opposite side of the net. Smiling, Roger ask, "Do you think that's a good place for the target?" and Percy would study it for a few seconds before it dawned on him that the target had to be on the same side as the ball machine. It became a standing joke between the two of them.

"Where do you put the target, Percy?"

"Duh, I don't know," and they laughed.

Boyer tells of one event that illustrates the effectiveness of their partnership as well as Percy's skill at salvaging difficult situations. In 1987, before hip surgery, Roger and Percy conducted a camp at Myr Mar Resort on Lake Mille Lacs. It was a two-day camp attended by 100 players. After the first hour of the first day, rain drove them inside. Undaunted, the two men set up tennis courts in the resort ballroom with chairs as net posts and boundaries and ropes for nets. They completed a full teaching schedule over two days using foam balls, and ran a doubles tournament with two divisions. In spite of the rain, the players learned what they came to learn and got more than their money's worth. "For introducing the game to seniors Percy is the best. He's an ambassador of the sport," Roger proclaimed.

In an article in the *Star Tribune* on March 3, 1987, Jim Fuller quoted Percy. "Tennis does a lot for elderly people who have lost loved ones, suffered griefs. The Lord has given me words, somehow I help people enjoy themselves and that makes me feel good."

In an interview with Steve Devich and Pam Dmytrenko in *Out and About in Richfield*, Percy said that his teaching technique emphasizes "short ground strokes, shoulder turn, racket back, and stepping through the ball." His trademark mantra to all has always been, "No foot faults." For backhand he emphasizes "racquet back, full swing, left hand guides racket." A review celebrating Percy as an honored alumnus of Minneapolis Central High School, quotes Percy about his teaching style: "Teach old and young with patience, empathy, and compassion. Teach each according to their physical ability...teach what the body can handle."

In that same review, Marci Bach, Executive Director of the USTA/Northern Section, commented about Percy, "He's a wonderful volunteer and has tremendous passion for the game. You won't meet anyone with a bigger heart than Percy Hughes. Just the mention of his name brings a smile to everyone's face. He's one of the greatest people I've known." Percy worked with her on the Community Development Committee for more than six years. He also developed a multicultural tennis program at the Minneapolis Indian Center. He has Cherokee blood in his veins from his father's side, and he felt a strong connection to the people he worked with there. He was happy to be included in their religious ceremonies.

Percy also started a non-profit, inner city tennis program, volunteering his time to teach kids. His purpose was "to build character, competence, and commitment to personal and community improvement." Monthly, he shared his tennis wisdom in the Senior Tennis Players newsletter *Senior Tennis Times* in his column, "Percy's Tennis Rhythms" that ended with his mantra, "No Foot Faults." Tennis has allowed Percy to be the athlete, the teacher, and the community servant, all of which suit his character.

17

"Broken Branches"

In 1991 Red Wolfe, Percy's best friend and musical partner, took ill with lung cancer. Red had always been a heavy smoker and loved a glass of bourbon or two, though never to excess. Eventually these habits destroyed his health. When Red was in treatment in Fairview Hospital, Percy visited him faithfully. His quartet even played at the hospital.

As Red's health deteriorated, he was transferred to St. Regent Hospital in Shakopee where he remained until his final days. Percy remembers coming to visit on September 18, 1991 to find an empty room. As he left the room, he saw Red lying on a cart, still. Percy was furious. "Red is deceased. How come he's lying on that cart?" he fumed at the closest nurse in sight. The indignity of it was too much for him. He thought about Red's gentle manner with his band men, his protection and caring for the younger sidemen such as trombonist Dave Graf and trumpeter Steve Wright, his resonant speaking voice as he introduced the numbers, and his sense of humor. He thought about how on the band stand Red joked with the audience that Percy was older than he—a full thirteen days older. Now he lay motionless on a cart in the hallway. It wasn't right. Percy vowed he would keep Red's memory and his music alive.

Shortly thereafter Red's wife Marlys passed away. The Wolfe children, Rick, Loren, and Amy, gave Percy the many charts Red had transcribed for the band. With those charts and fond memories of Red's music, Percy led the Red Wolfe Echoes of Ellington Memorial Band for the next eleven years.

At the time of Red's death, the entire jazz community was overcome with grief for this fine musician, band leader, composer, and stellar human being. On November 10 a benefit for the Jazz Society took place at the Hall Brothers' Jazz Emporium in Mendota Heights filling three stages in the Main Room, the Lounge, and the Dining Room with music all day and into the night. Ensembles such as the Wolverines, the Port of Dixie Memorial Band, the Red Wolfe Ellington Echoes Memorial Band, Barbary Coast, the Hall Bros, the Mouldy Figs, Percy Hughes Quartet, Reuben Ristrom, Eddie Tolck, Irv Williams, and performers Minnesota Dixie, Jeanne Arland Peterson, and Morris Wilson all offered tributes in their own inimicable styles. At 10 p.m. musicians in all three rooms cut loose in a jam. So ended the tribute, but not the memory, of Red Wolfe.

Although Percy became the leader of the Red Wolfe Memorial Ellington Echoes Band, he was not entirely comfortable in the role. According to some, Percy was happiest when he played with Red, the man and musician he most admired. As band leader, Percy found that making the arrangements for a performance demanded an attention to detail he would rather leave to someone else. He demanded perfection and got it, but not without anxiety to a fault. When the band played, however, the inner-turmoil subsided and Ellington's music and Red Wolfe's arrangements poured forth like vintage wine.

A life of fame, if not fortune, is often not what it seems. How many times we assume the icon is the reality—or at least want it to be for our inspiration and entertainment. Behind his winning smile and personality, Percy had grieved the loss of his wife, Judy, and his father, Percy, Sr. When he found Dee, joy returned to his life. Together they merged two families and lived happily, though misfortune paid them another visit in 1986 when Dee's grandmother, a delightful ninety-six year old who called Percy "My Boy," passed away at the Westwood Nursing Home where Dee worked. The next year Dee's mother, who had suffered through radiation for breast cancer, died during a procedure that burned her heart.

During their early years of marriage, Percy suffered hip pain. Shortly after undergoing hip replacement surgery in 1987, Dee's brother Bill died. Percy continued playing and instructing tennis until that same hip gave out completely in 1992. The surgeon rebuilt the shattered femur and once again replaced the hip. In 2000 Percy had the other one replaced, after which he returned to the tennis court as soon as the pain would allow. Today he walks gingerly but with determination. Nothing prevents him from following his passions: music, tennis, and family.

In 1993, Percy's mother, Virginia, died of congestive heart failure and chronic pulmonary disease. During her decline she lived at the Long Lake Nursing Home in a private room to accommodate her TV and snoring. She had a beautiful room, always decorated with flowers and a life-size Percy Hughes Main Street Jazz poster. Two large windows, stacks of newspapers, and family photo albums helped her to feel at home.

Virgie continued to be a woman of resolve until the end. She insisted upon her needs and care. Her way of doing things was the only way. Dee, for example, was not allowed to remove old newspapers and magazines or rearrange or, heaven forbid, discard rancid food from the refrigerator. The nurse would conspire with Dee for refrigerator clean out when Virgie was in the bath tub.

Once, when Virgie discovered that Dee had taken out her laundry, she scolded her so harshly that Dee said, "All right, if you don't want me to help you, I'll leave," and she turned toward the door.

But Virgie caught her up short, "Sit down," she ordered, "you know I love you, but I am mad at you."

Even her son couldn't escape her wrath. When Percy gathered up some old newspapers to discard, Virgie yelled, "Don't touch my papers. Get out. Get out." So Percy left for the moment. Still, Percy and Dee traveled daily from St. Louis Park to Long Lake to visit Virgie for two years. The day she died Percy was having his car serviced. He knew his mother lay near death and insisted that the service man hurry, to no avail. When Percy finally arrived at the nursing home, Virgie had passed away quietly.

Percy lost Louise, his first wife and mother of his children, to cancer in 1994. Because Dee, too, had lost both her parents, the two became patriarch and matriarch of their two families.

The next year Percy himself was diagnosed with prostate cancer. From January through March 1995 he drove every morning to the Hubert Humphrey Cancer Center at North Memorial Hospital in Robbinsdale for radiation treatments—thirty-nine in all. Often after treatment he would stop at Chuck Violette Park and muse. Then he'd drive to Normandale Community College to practice at 9 a.m. with the band. He never missed therapy and he never missed band. After the radiation therapy he continued with Lupron therapy to reduce the growth of any left over cancer cells.

But the most devastating event in Percy's personal life occurred in 1995 when Dee, attending a graduation party for Jenny Pendy at Bernice Pendy's home, saw the furniture spinning and flying across her vision. Sitting beside her daughter, Terry, she muttered, "I can't see. Something is wrong." Terry wanted to take her to the hospital immediately, but she said, "No, I'll be all right. I'll go home after the party." Her grandson, Chad, drove her home as she requested.

By the time she arrived, she could make out images, but headaches had started, followed by nausea. The next morning she called Dr. Brooks who ordered her to the hospital right away. The MRI showed bleeding from an aneurism in the frontal lobe of her brain. Three different surgeons agreed that surgery was impossible given the location and extent of the aneurism. Upon advice, Percy and Dee sought out Dr. Roberto Heroes, a brain surgeon specialist from Argentina, at the University of Minnesota. He studied the MRI and offered two options. Another surgeon performed the first by inserting a coil through a vein into the brain to break up clots and cauterize the lesion. The surgery failed. In fact, the surgeon announced to the family while Dee was still in the operating room that she wouldn't recover. Somehow she did.

In her hospital bed, she listened as Dr. Heroes asserted that he would perform the second option, brain surgery. He promised, "You will be okay." During the surgery she had a stroke that left her legs numb and impaired her speech, but somehow a flow of blood dissolved the clots and cleansed the aneurism. Father Smith at Dee's bedside reported that Heroes told him "No one can take credit for this but God."

"Do you have an angel?" Father Smith asked her.

"Yes, I do," she replied with impaired speed.

"Does your angel have a name?"

"No"

"He does now. It's Flo."

"Yes, it's Flo," she nodded.

From that time on Dee has sent Flo to help her friends in need.

After years of therapy Dee has overcome the speech impairment and numbness.

In 1996 Percy and Dee moved to the Edinborough condo where they lived for six years. Two years later Dee received a call from her son's friend who explained that Chuck had died in his sleep while taking an afternoon nap after work. Chuck's son, Shawn, arrived home from school, saw him on the couch and assumed he was asleep. As usual he changed clothes and went outside to play. When Chuck's live-in friend arrived from work, she noticed he wasn't breathing. The cause of death according to the autopsy report was either sleep apnea or heart failure. At his funeral, more friends and family arrived to pay their respects than the funeral home could accommodate. He was 38.

Percy had a third hip replacement in 2000, which made it nearly impossible to negotiate the many steps leading up to their condo. Later that year they moved to their current residence in Gramercy Park in Richfield. A few months later Percy's brother Clayton was diagnosed with pancreatic cancer. He suffered for six months, spending the last month in hospice at a private facility on Twin Lakes in Robbinsdale. On June 14, 2001, he passed away with Dee and Percy at his side. Percy was grief-stricken. Clayton and he were harmonious spirits. From the time they first played duets through the years of entertaining together at family gatherings, fishing the waters of Fish Lake and Lake Mille Lacs, smacking the ball over the net on the tennis court, these two were inseparable in spirit. His loss left a deep wound that has never healed.

But the couple faced more grief. In 2005 Kathleen, Dee's daughter, died of lung cancer. It is not intended that parents sit by the bedside of a dying child. How does one mend the heart from such a tear? How does one cope with so much loss: the deaths of Judy, a 96-year-old grandmother, a father, two mothers, two brothers, a close personal friend, a daughter, and the mother of his children? Then the personal health issues, a near fatal aneurism for Dee, hip replacements followed by rehabilitation and radiation treatments for prostate cancer for Percy.

Percy and Dee have learned to cope with such losses, supported by their Christian faith and the firm belief in the goodness of life. They continue to do what they love: music, tennis, baseball for Percy, volunteering for Dee. They look to the future, alive with possibilities. They don't try to understand why they have lost so much, only that they have. What matters is each other, sharing their gifts. Though a pervasive sadness lives deep within them, they act out the promise of life in every note played, every gesture of kindness, every sharing of knowledge. The teacher, the musician, the befriender, the volunteer exploring what is in them to do.

18

Looking Out Through the Leaves

After his hip replacements, Percy played his sax for a three-part series of video tapes produced by Fairview Riverside Medical Center and the Minnesota Joint Replacement Center called "Taking It All In Stride." He was also interviewed for the program. (Having had three hip-replacement operations himself, Percy was something of an expert.) This series, designed to educate and give assurance to those about to undergo a replacement, focused on preparation, precedures, and recovery with the help of patients who had been through it all. Photogenic and personable Percy lit up the screen.

In the TPT production of "The Lost Twin Cities II" that aired on March 6, 1995, Percy spoke about the jazz scene. A few years later he was interviewed briefly at the State Fair by Phil Johnson and Belinda Jensen of Channel 11 about black ball-players of the past. Percy had managed to foul off a couple of the fast balls from Satchel Paige during his Army years, and expressed the view that the Afro-American baseball players of the distant past had still not received their due. He cited Josh Gibson, who sent 32 balls over the fence in 1932 in the Negro League, as a case in point.

He and his Ellington Echoes Memorial Band were featured several times in the "Jazz Notes," the newletter of the Twin

Cities Jazz Society. In the October 2002 issue he wrote a tribute to "Pooper" or "The Professor," his nicknames for his friend and drummer Bob Pope who had passed away the previous August. It was Bob, Percy said, that steered him away from smoking and drinking in the '50's. "He was my role model, a man who taught me to avoid the pitfalls of the nightlife in the music business." As a past president of the exclusive Evergreen Music Educators Club, an organization of selected musicians that provided scholarships to young players, Percy played a rendition of "Body and Soul" in Bob's honor that Dennis Scholtes said was the most soulfully delivered performance of that tune he had ever heard.

Percy played with and served on the board of JazzMN, a nonprofit organization that promotes jazz by sponsoring concerts and working with young people in the schools to preserve jazz history. He was an organizing member of the Twin Cities Jazz Society and was featured with his band many times at their "Jazz from J to Z" events. For example, his quintet, with Mel Carter on trumpet and Shirley Witherspoon as vocalist, played for the fifteenth anniversary of the Jazz Society at the Chattanooga Music Cafe in Bandana Square on February 15, 1994, in honor of Black History Month. Other groups at this event included the Irv Williams Quintet, and the pianists Jimmy Hamilton and Rufus Webster, with Doris Hines singing. Also the James (Cornbread) Harris Quintet performed. The event paid homage to such fine black musicians as Dr. Reginald Buchner, and also to local musicians who hit the big scene, Oscar Pettiford and Lester Young. In July of 1994, Hearing Aide of Minnesota sponsored several ensembles including the Kenwood Chamber Ensemble and the Cyril Paul Band that joined the Percy Hughes Quartet with Shirley Witherspoon at the Calhoun Beach Club.

A month later, on a bright, warm Thursday afternoon, Percy led the Red Wolfe Ellington Echoes Memorial Band for a "Jazz on the Mall" concert at the patio of the Minneapolis Public

Percy with longtime accompanist Nancy Lovgren

Library. On these gigs Tim Sullivan delighted the audience on the trumpet and Bill Barber offered his artistry on the piano.

At South High he and his quartet offered a "Jazz is Cool" program and invited student musicians to sit in with them. He did a similar gig at Risen Christ Catholic School for young children and conducted Jazz Master Workshops at 46th and Chicago. His group played for the Freedom Festival at Minnehaha Falls in 2001 and another Jazz from J to Z at the Artists' Quarter in St. Paul in 2002. Several times his band played "Music in the Parks," sponsored by the Hopkins Center for the Arts directed by Jim Shirley. He joined local musicians at the Arrowhead Center for the Arts in Grand Marais and at the Art Center in Fergus Falls. Always his motive was to entertain and teach. His Ellington Echoes Band was the main attraction at the Reed Sweatt Tennis Center fund raiser in October of 2002 where he brought his music and tennis together.

Percy and Nancy Lovgren also found the time to slip in an hour here and there for birthdays and anniversaries. Once on November 12, 2000, they made a guest appearance in the Gallery for a "Sounds Good to Me: Music in Minnesota" performance at the Minnesota Historical Society for which they receive many accolades.

The gigs for the Hopkins Center for the Arts brought musicians and organizers together into a social network. Jim Shirley, chair of the Hopkins Performing Arts Committee, booked Percy and the Ellington Echoes for his "Music in the Park" series, on the advice of Jim Fuller, a friend from school days and reporter and editor for the *Minneapolis Star Tribune*. This series included well-known artists such as vibraphonist and pianist Terry Gibbs and keyboardist Dick Hyman. The musicians and committee members gathered after the concert for a bite to eat and a chat about the music scene. Soon such gatherings became a habit that included wives or significant others. The entourage included Percy and Dee, Jim and Mary Shirley, Jim and Lee Fuller, and Don Holton, a tennis friend of Percy with his friend, Ann Evans. Since one couple each month chose the venue, the group tasted fine cuisine all over the city. Once Jim and Mary Shirley invited the eightsome to their cabin on Ottertail Lake for the weekend—a trip that included a fine dinner at Stubb's or Pier One. Soon the summer gathering at the lake became a standing event.

In a telephone interview Jim Shirley recreated the image of Percy, eager and prepared with the latest fishing paraphenalia, sitting in the bow of the boat as it skimmed over the water from one fishless spot to another, singing "O Solo Mio" at the top of his lungs. Nothing has meant more to Percy and Dee than the joie d' vive they experience with their friends.

Percy's jazz career reached a climax of sorts on November 9, 2002, when the Normandale Creative Arts Series sponsored a celebration of Duke Ellington's music. Ellington made more than 150 recordings in his career and composed close to 800 songs. The event, billed as a fund-raiser for students in need, featured Percy leading the Red Wolfe Memorial 'Echoes of Ellington' Octet, along with a choice set of film-clips of Ellington

Your "Echoes" entertainers...

The movies & the music of	The Octet of	The films of
Duke Ellington	**Percy Hughes**	**Bob DeFlores**

himself chosen by Bob DeFlores from his renowned film archive. The musicians playing with Percy that night were Jim TenBensel, trombone; Steve Wright, trumpet; Russ Peterson, saxes and clarinet; Jimmy Hamilton, piano; Jerry Burton, drums; Al Closmore, guitar; and Gordy Johnson, bass. The program included vocal renditions of "Sophisticated Lady" and "Satin Doll" by Geoff Jones and the Ellington Echoes band playing, "Squeeze Me," "The Mooch," "That's the Blues, Old Man," "Good Queen Bess," and "Don't Get Around Much Anymore." The music served as a fitting tribute not only to the Duke but also to Red Wolfe and Percy Hughes, whose talent had been so vital to the jazz community for over 60 years. This gala event may well have been the end of an era.

During many years in the limelight Percy enjoyed favorable reviews, not only from reporters, but also from his audience and sidemen. Did Percy ever have disagreements with band members? Of course. But not once in the many interviews I've conducted with musicians, tennis players, union members, and students, have I heard an unkind word about him. Dave Graf, who took Gene Bird's place in the Echoes in 1987 and played with the band for 11 years, remarked, "Percy is a warm, wonderful person, a dapper man. He's totally reliable; people love him; he's a generous and giving man." He recalled that Percy loved to scat on "A Train" and had "Satin Doll" on his answering machine at home. "He was one of kind," Dave said. The accolades go on and on from Leigh Kamman, Alan Lotsberg, Douglas Snapps, Dick Bortolucci, Reuben Ristrom, Dennis Scholtes, Nancy Lovgren, Carl Carlson, Russ Peterson, Jim Fuller, Roger Boyer, Marci Bach and from his wife Dee and son, Percy III and daughter, Cheryl, and all the grandchildren.

Beyond these friends and musicians stretches Percy's greater influence—those he taught in high school and college classrooms, those he coached at Reed Sweatt and the dozens of tennis courts around the state, and those who came to hear him play and to dance to his music for more than sixty years.

Percy has received many awards as a result of these efforts. There are three that deserve special mention. The first is the Community Connection Award he received on April 12, 2003 from Normandale Community College. For a week before this gala event, college planners contacted Percy's wife Dee to accumulate the data for a video review of Percy's many contributions in music, tennis, and education. Dee snuck around Percy like a weasel, all smiles and deception, a role she was unaccustomed to playing. She funneled photos, video clips, news releases, thank you notes and letters to Normandale's media department, where the video was produced with the able assistance of film archivist, Bob DeFlores, all without Percy's suspicion. He knew he was to be honored on the designated night but had no idea of the extent or exclusiveness of the award. He was the fifth to receive this honor, joining Charlie Boone and Roger Erickson, the international futurist Earl Jacobs, and film archivist Bob DeFlores. The task of gathering and organizing material for the film would have been far more difficult, were it not for the fact that Dee had been sorting Percy's memorabilia for years, arranging it into scrapbooks in chronological order.

On the night of the event, the whole family—Percy III,

133

Cheryl, Dee's Terry and Toni and all the grandchildren—arrived in their finest evening attire for the occasion. Percy, too, at Dee's behest wore a tux.

The event was entitled, "French Quarter on France Avenue, honoring Twin Cities Legend, Percy Hughes." At 6 p.m. the Ariel Trio played for the pre-prandial social and silent auction. The dinner and program, which commenced at 7:30, was catered by Bayou Bob's. The Ragin' Cajun Menu consisted of andouille sausage en croute, zydeco artichoke with Port Salut, fire-roasted cajun shrimp, bourbon beef brochette for appetizers and tasso pork with jambalaya pasta, sweet potato pepper pecan salad blended in cinnamon vinaigrette, blackened beef medallion and cajun catfish with roasted corn mashed potato and plantation vegetables...and for dessert, apricot nectar cake with chocolate almond swirl. Geoff Jones and Ginger Commodore provided the dinner entertainment. Obviously,  this was not your typical after-church Sunday dinner of roast beef, potatoes and gravy, green beans, and vanilla ice cream. It was a banquet for an extraordinary person.

Alan Lotsberg was emcee for the after-dinner program. Normandale President Dr. Thomas J. Horak offered the welcome. The Normandale Chorus sang and the Nujazz Trio performed. Then Bob DeFlores and the Normandale media department rolled out the video projector.

Family members reminisced on-screen about the 78 rpm records of Duke Ellington's band that Percy's mother played time and time again. Long-time friends and supporters such as Leigh Kamman looked back on Percy's early career, describing it as "pace setting, innovative, original, new." "His octet," Kamman said, "sounded like a fifteen or eighteen piece band." Russ

Peterson added that after the entry, 'good guy,' in the dictionary, one ought to find the name, Percy Hughes. Bob DeFlores noted that his musical accomplishments aside, Percy had a huge impact on the children he worked with in the schools. Pete Cameron from the Jazz Society called him an admirable beloved person, and a gift to the community.

Percy responded, "This tribute is unbelievable. I'm in awe... I'm a people person. Love your brothers and sisters. It's the way I was brought up." Then Dr. Horak and Larry Jodsaas, NCCF Board President, presented Percy with the 2003 Community Connections Award. At that point Percy uncased his saxophone and performed for an evening of music and dancing.

Later that year Percy received a second impressive honor. On November 1, at the Holiday Inn Select in Bloomington, Minnesota, Percy, along with twelve others, was inducted into the Northern Section Tennis Hall of Fame at a dinner ceremony recognizing his contributions to the world of tennis. Percy had received the Senior Tennis Hall of Fame Award for Minnesota in 1988, an award based on not only "skill and reputation, but also continued activity and inspiration to the million senor tennis players in the USA." Now the honor was being expanded to encompass the Northern Section of the USTA.

The third award arrived unexpectedly in 2008. One day, after arriving home from band practice at Normandale, Percy received a call from Fred Jurecwicz.

"Percy, you have been selected by USTA for the 2007 Senior Service Award."

"Really, what does that mean?"

"It means you will be transported by NWA to Naples, Florida, for a three-day all-expenses-paid trip, where you will be handed the award by the President of USTA in front of all the tennis dignitaries."

There was a long pause.

"They selected me?"

"Yes, for your, and I quote, 'your willingness, cooperation, and participation in Senior Tennis.'"

"Wow, I'm amazed. I can't believe it."

"They'll ask you to make a brief acceptance speech."

"Well, you know I can do that. I have many to thank, like Mike Goldhammer, Dave Matthews, Marie Thompson, and Ernie Green. You know Ernie gave me tennis lessons. And wow. That's all I can say, Wow."

Percy and Dee flew to Naples to receive the award. He had seldom traveled beyond the borders of Minnesota, and both the trip and the award were adventures of a lifetime.

Percy and Dee with the Senior Service tennis award.

In his acceptance speech he thanked his friends, mentors, and wife, Dee, and the many people who had been so kind and generous to him.

"I love you guys," he said.

That expression may well define Percy's feelings about most of the people with whom he has worked in music, tennis, education, and postal delivery. He has always treated others with respect and kindness, because he believes in the worth of every human being. There's a humility about him that all the rave revues, awards, and personal tributes have not diminished. While he knows his best is good, he also admires the talent of fellow musicians. He has never aspired to the "big time"; he has never intentionally set out to make a name for himself. He's never quite believed he could play baseball with Jackie Robinson or sax with Johnny Hodges, but many think he could have. The reviews attest to that.

He didn't take over the leadership of his first band in 1946;

he was elected. While his name was on the marquis for every engagement, he honored his sidemen. He was honored to play for Red Wolfe's Ellington Echoes Band, and after Red's passing, he took over the lead without changing the name much: Red Wolfe's Ellington Echoes Memorial Band. In time, as his career progressed, his name brought the crowd. And that, too, was a good thing, because what mattered was that people heard and enjoyed the music. He has always wanted to be part of people's lives, entertaining them, sharing what he knew, never saying, "Look at me," but rather "Listen to the music," "Pat yourself on the back," "You can do it."

When Percy first climbed the elm tree in his backyard, he discovered that the climb was more important than reaching the top. Later he discovered that it wasn't even the climb that mattered, but living among the branches and leaves. Some of the branches broke. Sometimes he fell and felt the wounds, but found his place again among the branches of that childhood tree. "It's time to practice," his mother called to him. He didn't know it then, but that was the trunk of the tree he would climb for the rest of his life.

The expression "No regrets" often means to avoid dwelling on past mistakes. And Emerson once said that "the reward of a thing well done is to have done it." Both perspectives focus on today and tomorrow, rather than yesterday. Those that make the best of today build a future and establish themselves in the present. That's what Percy has done. That's his legacy. That's the stuff of legend.

From time to time I become aware of things going on right under my nose that I hadn't noticed, such as a new building under construction that finally catches my attention when the sun glares at me from one of its windows, or a barber shop in a nearby shopping mall that goes out of business that I didn't know existed. Or that Percy Hughes' Band, one of the most respected jazz ensemble in the Twin Cities, had been playing at The Point a mile from my house for seventeen years without ever capturing my attention. Only now, in later life, have I come to know this humble, talented, and extraordinary human being. To this I say, "No regrets," but I also say, "I wish I had been there."

On April 9, 2010, Percy Hughes turned eighty-eight. Besides the family celebration, the Normandale Community College band members signed a card, took photos, and presented Percy with a cake. He was nearing his twenty-fourth year with the band. During reheasal Jim Kurschner, director, congratulated him and thanked him for his years of service and dedication to the band.

At the April 29th band concert, Kurschner dedicated Robert Russell Bennett's "American Suite" to Percy Hughes who was too ill to play the concert. He spoke of Percy's musicianship, his awards, his dedication, and his mentoring of students over the years, a fine tribute to the man who had never missed a concert and tried as hard as he could not to miss this one. On the previous Saturday, the 24th, he was rushed to Fairview South Hospital to stop the flow of a ruptured ulcer. When the bleeding was

Percy with Jim Kurschner.

under control and the test results were evaluated, it was determined that Percy had stomach cancer. The surgery took place the following Friday. It went well although it was necessary to remove two-thirds of his stomach. After a few days in the hospital and several weeks convalescing at the Masonic Rehabilitation Center in Bloomington, Percy returned home. Slowly, he regained his strength until by late August he was ready to drive himself to Normandale Community College to play his alto sax with the band again. After his diagnosis few thought he would ever play again. But Percy thought otherwise; he never gave up. He never has. Don't be surprised if he shows up at Reed Sweatt, tennis racket in hand, ready to offer a few tips.

SELECTED AWARDS

- May 12, 1982, received the Black Music Award created by Pete Rhodes and associates to honor black musicians of Minnesota descent
- 1983, received the Minnesota Black Music Award for Lifetime Achievement
- 1985—Percy and Red Wolfe received certificate of commendation from Gov. Rudy Perpich for keeping jazz alive
- 1985—Mayors George Latimer and Don Frazer proclaimed Nov. 16 the Red Wolfe and Percy Hughes Day in the Twin Cities
- 1987—inducted into the Minnesota Jazz Hall of Fame
- 1988—second recipient of the Jack Dow Senior Development Award for coaching senior tennis
- 1996—inducted into the MN Music Hall of Fame
- 2000—received the William Griffin Performing Arts Award
- 2003—inducted into the USTA Northern Hall of Fame
- 2004—received with Leigh Kamman the Lifetime Achievement Award from Walker West Music Academy
- 2007—received USTA Senior Service Award, in Naples, Florida

About the Author

Jim Swanson taught American Literature, composition, and creative writing to high school students for thirty-five years. In 1978 he authored a creative writing teaching package published by EMC titled: *Creative Writing: The Whole Kit and Caboodle*. Since retirement he has revived his musical gifts and now plays in two concert bands, a Dixieland band, a jazz quintet and a woodwind quintet.